A WORLD
WORTH
SAVING

A WORLD WORTH SAVING

LENTEN SPIRITUAL PRACTICES FOR ACTION

GEORGE HOVANESS DONIGIAN

UPPER
ROOM BOOKS®
NASHVILLE

Library of Congress Cataloging-in-Publication Data

Donigian, George Hovaness.
  A World Worth Saving: Lenten Spiritual Practices for Action / George Hovaness Donigian.
      pages cm
    ISBN 978-0-8358-1211-5 ISBN 978-0-8358-1212-2 ISBN 978-0-8358-1213-9
  1. Lent. 2. Christian life. 3. Spiritual life. I. Title.
  BV85.D617 2013
  248.4—dc23

                                                              2012046482

Printed in the United States of America

Little children, let us love,
not in word or speech, but in truth and action.

—1 John 3:18

CONTENTS

PREFACE

To SOME PEOPLE this book's content may seem elementary. *A World Worth Saving* looks at basic acts of mercy and justice and connects these outer actions with our inner practices of prayer, Bible reading, and the Lenten fast. I want to tell you how this book came to life, my intent for the book, and some alternate ways to use the book.

Let me begin by posing some questions:

- How do we connect public worship with what happens Tuesday afternoon at work or Thursday night at the retail outlet?
- How do we love God and love our neighbor?
- How do we live a life of Christian discipleship in a world that bases life on a cynical "Golden Rule"? (Variations on the rule include "the one who dies with the most toys wins" and "the one with the most gold makes the rules.")

As we struggle with these questions, we may also ask the following:

- When and where do we experience grace?
- When do we receive love and when do we give it?

I ask myself those questions daily. I come honestly to these questions. Several different traditions inform my understanding of Christian discipleship. I participate in the life of The United Methodist Church and am a Methodist because of my desire to be saved from my sins and to grow in love with God and neighbor. I was baptized in the Armenian Apostolic Orthodox Church. Later, a neighbor took my brother and me to Sunday school at a congregation of the Lutheran Church—Missouri Synod, where I was confirmed in the body of Christ. Immediately after that, I became a thirteen-year-old cadet at Fork Union Military Academy, a school related to the Virginia Southern Baptist Convention and a place where I experienced much law and little grace. I then went to a small liberal arts college in Georgia where faculty and staff members offered encouragement in my attaining a liberal arts education. After college, members of the faculty of the Candler School of Theology at Emory University fostered more questions about Christian spiritual practices and public witness. While I honor these different church traditions, I also hold a Wesleyan perspective on God's abundant grace. As many others before me, I practice and teach John Wesley's General Rules: to do no harm, to do good inasmuch as possible, and to observe the basic Christian practices that open us to God's grace: participating in public worship, frequent Communion, daily Bible reading, daily prayer, fasting, and Christian conferencing.

I hold a running conversation in my journal: How am I growing in love with God? How did I engage in Christian mission? How does Sunday worship connect with what I do throughout the week?

Those actions—both the outward actions and my silent reflection—all seem to point to the inner life, but my inner life is not the life anyone sees. How do I witness to others? I could, for example, fast for the season of Lent. In the Armenian tradition worshipers fast not only for Lent but also for the forty days of Advent. In the traditional fast we do not eat meat or animal products. Fasting allows us to focus more of our thoughts on God's grace. But something within me continues to raise questions about Christian witness. I feel a need to go beyond the seasonal disciplines to think more seriously about my actions. I am not alone in asking questions. Pope Leo I (Leo the Great) addressed questions about fasting in a sermon during his pontificate. Leo's papacy began on September 29, 440, and lasted more than twenty years until his death on November 10, 461. Leo addressed a concern for the Advent fast in this way:

> What can be more useful than fasting? By that exercise we draw near to God, we make strong stand against the devil, and overcome the sweet enticements of sin. Fasting has ever been the bread of strength. . . .
> But since fasting is not the only means to secure health for our souls, let us adorn our fasting with works of mercy. Spend in good deeds what you withdraw from superfluity. Our fast must be turned into a banquet for the poor. Let us devote time and effort to the underprivileged, the widow and the orphan; let us show sympathy to the afflicted and reconcile the estranged; provide lodging for the wanderer and relieve the oppressed; give clothing to the naked and cherish the sick.[1]

Adorning our fast with works of mercy and justice, as Pope Leo said, remains a significant part of our spiritual journey today for two reasons. The first reason concerns the way our actions match and mirror our confession of faith. We follow Jesus Christ who offered mercy and compassion to all people and who taught about God's justice.

The second reason goes to the heart of our understanding of God's incarnation in Christ. *A World Worth Saving* is not simply a book title; the phrase grows from our faith. We believe that God loves the world so deeply that God became human like us in the person of Jesus. We believe that God redeems the world out of divine love. We further believe that God not only loves the world but believes in its value and worth. The Creator surrounds us with love and extends grace to us and all people because God believes we are worthy of redemption. We act in concert with God to extend grace, mercy, and love to all whom God values.

I hope you will learn ways to adorn your fasting with works of mercy and discover how you can better connect your inner life with your external actions. This book will introduce you to people who have influenced and shaped me as a "liberal evangelical," a term I use to avoid being pigeonholed in a theological category and therefore dismissed. Among its definitions, *liberal* means "generous." For me, *evangelical* refers to Jesus' proclamation of the kingdom of God—in Greek, *euangelion* or good news. You and I can offer generous good news to a world in need. For this gift, we join in thanksgiving to God.

Reading and Using This Book

Why would I want to tell you how to read this book? Read the book by yourself. Reading is a solitary act, but every book also invites us to share from it. We do this as often as we read a book and recommend it to a friend or talk about how difficult the book seemed. *A World Worth Saving* extends the invitation to share content—but in a different way. The book calls for action. The places where we live demand different responses as we think about hospitality or hunger. Ministry in the urban core of Philadelphia, Pennsylvania, differs from ministry in Kilmarnock, Virginia. The needs of a rural community in Illinois differ from the needs of a rural community in California. You provide the follow-up to the direction noted in this book. You will discover new ways to expand the love of God in your community.

A World Worth Saving offers daily reflection exercises and questions. Some of the exercises repeat themselves because we learn best through repetition. Through repetition we delve into a subject and formulate new responses. As you read and reflect on particular topics, you may desire to converse with others in your community who share a passion for justice and mercy. Others in your church or community may only need a nudge to join a group in acting.

You may choose to read the book as part of a group study. An accountability and mission group may read the book together and ascertain new strengths for mission or give birth to a *new* mission group as like-minded individuals attempt to extend God's justice in the community.

In addition to the reflection questions and exercises, I offer some resource recommendations. These recommendations take different forms: books, websites, and videos.

Another item of note: You will find brief sections marked An Interruption in several weeks. The information in these sections seemed helpful to include though not necessarily a part of the week's flow. For example, one interruption describes the work of chimney sweeps because that information provides background to understanding the writer of a nineteenth-century hymn. I hope you will enjoy these background moments.

After reading each chapter, take time to begin reflection on the Day 1 exercise. The next day take time to reflect on the Day 2 exercise and follow the guidance that comes with each day. Each day links with the previous reflection and action exercise. You will find these exercises particularly helpful for your congregation's ministry. You may choose to write full responses in a journal or make brief notes. If you meet with a group, feel free to bring your journal or notes to the group gathering and talk together about the nudges and ideas you have gained.

ACKNOWLEDGMENTS

I AM THANKFUL to Jeannie Crawford-Lee, editorial director of Upper Room Books, who in May 2012 asked me if I had any book ideas. I put together a proposal and waited. Upper Room Books accepted the proposal and with that came the work of completing the manuscript during the summer months. In addition to writing during the summer, my wife and I moved to a new city and new jobs at the end of June.

I am thankful to the people of Lupo Memorial United Methodist Church in Greenwood, South Carolina, who were around when the conversation about this project began, and to the people of Monaghan United Methodist Church in Greenville, South Carolina, who were patient during the writing.

Writing a book is a solitary project that involves a community. My community includes teachers and friends from many different chapters in life. Some are dead, but their presence remains with me. I thank the following members of that community:

Don Saliers for a friendship that began at the Candler School of Theology and has extended through many significant events. Don encouraged me to claim both the Armenian

Orthodox and Protestant theological traditions and the jazz and classical music traditions.

Reverend Father (or Der) Tateos Abdalian, coordinator of mission parishes for the Armenian Archdiocese, and traveling priest. Der Tateos demonstrates the warm heart of a Wesleyan and speaks Armenian with a hearty Boston accent.

Flora Slosson Wuellner, E. Glenn Hinson, and W. Paul Jones are authors with whom I have worked and who have continued the conversation in different ways.

Anita Flowers of Pinnacle Leadership Associates in South Carolina helped reawaken the writer within me after a long period of grief.

The late Dan U. Biggers, counselor, college dean, actor, and friend continues to inspire me.

I am thankful also to other friends from my Berry College days who enjoy and guard their privacy. These inspiring friends know who they are.

Van Quinn, a friend from my Fork Union Military Academy days, continues to show up at odd intervals in my life with encouragement.

Ginna Minasian Dalton and Susan Minasian, my cousins and sisters in ministry, have held me accountable for a lifetime.

And I thank Mary for all these reasons and many more.

The Armenian Feast of the Holy Cross
September 15, 2012

WEEK 1

Fasting from Apathy

Indeed, God did not send the Son into the world to condemn the world, but in order that the world might be saved through him.

—JOHN 3:17

As WE MOVE FROM Shrove Tuesday (Mardi Gras) to Ash Wednesday, we move from frivolity and celebration to a condition of spiritual preparation for Easter. Giving up something for Lent is a familiar tradition for many, a variation on an old and rich tradition of self-denial known as fasting. You may know someone like my friend Russ, an artist, who each year gives up liver for Lent. He does not eat liver any other time of the year, so his Lenten self-denial points to little sacrifice. Maybe you know people who approach the season of Lent by giving up chocolate or coffee or another indulgence and then follow through with that intention until Easter. The idea of giving up something—usually a personally meaning-ful practice or custom—for Lent has become *one* way to fast during the season. The reasoning behind this ancient tradition focused on ways to develop openness to God. The earliest tradition of Lenten fasting came in eating only flatbread and drinking only water in order to prepare spiritually with the understanding that the seasonal fast allowed more time to focus on the love of Christ through prayer and devotion and thus to celebrate Jesus' resurrection. Over the centuries this tradition has evolved into simple acts of self-denial.

An Interruption

Before we consider the importance of fasting in our journey as Christian disciples, I need to express a foundational belief because I do not want to make assumptions about others' faith or beliefs. As I read the Bible, I *always* see God acting on behalf of Creation by offering guidance, direction, and salvation. God offers salvation in the prehistory of Adam and Eve, the early history of Israel, and in the concerns of the prophets like Amos and Hosea. We see God's gift of salvation most fully in the person and work of Jesus Christ.

Why do you think God has constantly acted and continues to act on behalf of Creation and humanity?

We might answer this question by saying that God loves us, but I think we need to acknowledge a more basic truth: God believes the world is worth saving;

the world is worthy of redemption. John 3:17 states this essential truth: "'God did not send the Son into the world to condemn the world, but in order that the world might be saved through him.'" Remember this as we journey toward Easter.

Fasting

Eating and sleeping are normal human behaviors and basic to our existence! Thousands of years of human history tell us to *avoid* fasting. Genetics and grandmothers tell us to eat because we may need the stores of food within our bodies during the next famine. Dieters know that complete fasting does not help them lose weight because the body shuts down in order to preserve strength. Food is necessary even for the sake of dieting and weight loss.

Look with me at the season of Lent as a time when we take on a special fast in honor of Jesus and focus on the gifts God has given us through him. Our fast will move us closer to Jesus' ministry and mission and will encourage our spiritual growth. We will consider three primary reasons for fasting in the Bible and come to understand some connections between fasting and our attitudes toward life. We will move from the inner action of fasting to outward expressions of faith and discipleship. The fast to which I invite you is not a traditional fast from food or drink but a fast that takes us in an intentional direction. This fast will motivate us to put our inner faith and spiritual practice into action that demonstrates God's love and mercy for the world.

Fasting in the Bible

The Hebrew Bible notes several types of traditional fasts. No one thought of fasting as a way to lose weight. The first and, perhaps, only fast designated by the Law concerns Yom Kippur, the Day of Atonement (Lev. 16:29-31; Num. 29:7). Tradition calls for a fast beginning twenty minutes before sundown on the day before Yom Kippur until after nightfall the next day. A primary purpose for the fast is repentance and forgiveness for wrongs committed against God and creation. The dominant emotion during this time is one of grief. When people in the Bible grieved, they fasted. We see this in 2 Samuel 1:12 when David and his soldiers mourn the deaths of Saul and Jonathan. They tear their clothes, weep, and fast. Fasting is a normal part of life in the Bible, particularly when grieving, seeking God's blessings, or asking for forgiveness.

While this book does not survey the different types of fasting found in scripture, I do want to look at some examples briefly. Passages in the Hebrew scriptures speak of fasting as preparation for new ventures, for change, and for a deeper sense of God's presence. The most significant of these passages are Exodus 34:28 and Deuteronomy 9:18. These verses describe Moses fasting on Mount Sinai while he is with God and receives the Ten Commandments.

Jesus fasts several times in the Gospels. He fasts in the wilderness for forty days while facing temptation from Satan (see Matt. 4:1-11; Mark 1:12-13; Luke 4:1-13). Jesus' time of preparation and prayer prior to beginning his public ministry involves fasting. We do not see Jesus mourning or grieving here unless he mourns for the broken state of the world and its sin. We do not know why Jesus fasted prior to beginning his public ministry, but we believe that Jesus focused his prayers on his relationship with God and for the sake of his mission to the world. When Jesus prays in the garden of Gethsemane, we sense his concern for the world. I believe that his prayers in the garden are the culmination of his prayers begun in the wilderness. In Matthew 26 Jesus says to the disciples, "I am deeply grieved, even to death; remain here, and stay awake with me" (v. 38). Jesus then prays, "My Father, if it is possible, let this cup pass from me; yet not what I want but what you want" (v. 39). This prayer directs us to a deeper understanding of Jesus' purpose and his commitment. Jesus prays and fasts for himself, his followers, and for the world.

In the Sermon on the Mount, Jesus tells his followers to break with the common custom of putting ashes on one's body and face to signify the fast: "When you fast, put oil on your head and wash your face, so that your fasting may be seen not by others but by your Father who is in secret" (Matt. 6:17-18). From this, we infer that Jews during Jesus' time fasted, and he expected his followers to continue to fast—though not in ways that would draw attention to themselves.

Before Barnabas and Saul set out on their mission to Cyprus, the members of the church at Antioch fasted, prayed, and laid hands on them (Acts 13:1-3). When Saul and Barnabas entered the mission field and consecrated leaders, the churches employed the practices of prayer and fasting to entrust their leadership to the Lord (Acts 14:21-23). The epistles speak little about fasting, but the absence of references may indicate the matter-of-fact nature of fasting in the life of the early church.

I view fasting as a way to let go of our earthly cares for a time and to stand empty before God. I think of fasting as a way to imitate Jesus Christ in the wilderness. Throughout the history of the church, preachers and teachers have invited followers to have the mind and heart of Christ. Whether a simple sacrifice of some favorite food or an elaborately planned system of fasting, the invitation to imitate Christ calls for more than this action of giving up a food that we may or may not like. Our consideration of fasting will take us on a course of action that will make a difference during the season of Lent and well beyond Easter.

Apathy

In the 1950s people in Western cultures began using the term *compassion fatigue* to describe the overworked and overstressed nurses. Those who experience compassion fatigue feel hopeless in the face of daily challenges. Some people today think that the United States (and elsewhere) suffers from compassion fatigue because news outlets relay constant coverage of tragedies. Social scientists also point to the effects that constant appeals to donate money to multiple causes have on people. We also read and hear stories about financial malfeasance of directors or leaders of businesses and charitable organizations. This saturation of bad news, cynicism, and hopelessness seems to rule the world; we feel no desire to make a difference in it.

Even if we do not suffer from fully developed compassion fatigue, we often experience some degree of apathy. Those who feel apathy no longer exhibit interest or concern in social, spiritual, emotional, or physical life. They simply feel indifferent to life. This condition affects people of all faiths and beliefs and is not new. By the seventeenth century, the church called this indifference to life a spiritual sickness (*acedia*) and first identified the disease among monks who became unable to perform their duties. Centuries earlier, Thomas Aquinas related *acedia*—which he also described as "the sorrow of the world"—to sloth, one of the seven deadly sins. Theologians in the Middle Ages thought that not caring for the world, which they identified as sloth, led people to suicide—the gravest form of this spiritual illness.

Most of us do not experience apathy to this degree. We are just a *little* apathetic. We perceive the world as stacked against our efforts. Large corporations seem to care little about their impact upon the world beyond their own profits. We witness governments that cannot care for their needy and sputter to achieve peace and stability. We see cover-ups or schemes to hide their misconduct. We witness famine and genocide in other parts of the world and think, *The problems are so large that we cannot make a difference. Why try?*

The answer takes us back to my point: God thinks the world is worth saving. As followers of Jesus Christ, we believe that the world is worthy of redemption. We *can* and *do* make a difference in the world. Our caring actions help redeem the world. Together with God we provide necessary assistance, grow spiritually through mission, and demonstrate our belief in God's ongoing offer of salvation to the world.

A Prescription for Apathy

This Lenten season I invite you to break from the usual cus-tom of fasting or other form of self-denial and, instead, to fast from apathy. That means you set aside all your noncaring attitudes and move closer to the caring love of God. Even in its mildest form, apathy is a spiritual illness. The cure for apathy is also a spiritual one. We cannot give up apathy the way my friend gives up liver for Lent. We must move from prayer to action. Remember that the Israelites and people in biblical times fasted for three purposes: (1) forgiveness and reconciliation with God and with others, (2) grief, and (3) in preparation for deep spiritual experiences. They fasted to be open to God. Many of our world's conditions cause a bottomless grief and sorrow. We grieve these conditions because they show us the brokenness of our world.

What Wondrous Love Is This

Start by reading "What Wondrous Love Is This," a hymn sung in many churches during the season of Lent. The famous composer Anonymous receives credit for the words and the tune. According to William Walker, who collected Appalachian hymns during the early nineteenth century, a man named James Christopher of Spartanburg, South Carolina, brought together the words he heard in one unidentified community and a plaintive tune he heard in still another community. Neither William Walker nor James Christopher claimed credit for the words or the tune.

> What wondrous love is this, O my soul, O my soul,
> what wondrous love is this, O my soul!
> What wondrous love is this that caused the Lord of bliss
> to bear the dreadful curse for my soul, for my soul,
> to bear the dreadful curse for my soul.

What wondrous love is this, O my soul, O my soul,
what wondrous love is this, O my soul!
What wondrous love is this, that caused the Lord of life
to lay aside his crown for my soul, for my soul,
to lay aside his crown for my soul.

To God and to the Lamb I will sing, I will sing,
to God and to the Lamb, I will sing;
to God and to the Lamb who is the great I AM,
while millions join the theme I will sing, I will sing;
while millions join the theme I will sing.

And when from death I'm free, I'll sing on, I'll sing on,
and when from death I'm free, I'll sing on;
and when from death I'm free, I'll sing and joyful be,
and through eternity I'll sing on, I'll sing on,
and through eternity I'll sing on.

Our friend Anonymous knows how to describe the wonder of God's love and redemption. The hymn speaks of Christ's redemptive love. We read the words and experience a sense of awe as we contemplate Jesus' sacrificial love. We gain a sense of timelessness in God—past, present, and future become one as we sing praise for Christ's ongoing redemption of the world. When I think of the roots of this hymn, I am drawn to Philippians 2:5-11. Here we read how Christ, though equal to God, humbled and emptied himself to become a slave. He obeyed God even to the point of death on the cross. The biblical hymn concludes with verses of praise and exaltation that every knee on heaven and earth and under the earth should bend and "every tongue should confess that Jesus Christ is Lord" (Phil. 2:10-11). Such is the praise of the Philippians hymn and also the praise of "What Wondrous Love Is This."

I invite you to notice a peculiarity in this hymn from Anonymous: There are no question marks. We might expect to see a question mark at the end of a sentence that begins with *What*. Throughout the hymn we sing one declarative statement after another. Each stanza praises God for the gift of Christ. This steadfast declaration of faith invites us to ask one question: Why did Jesus Christ empty himself or, as the hymn says, "bear the dreadful curse for my soul"?

The answer: God thinks that the world is worth saving and invites us to believe this too. If we, like Jesus Christ, believe the world is worth saving, then we will act on behalf of Christ for the sake of the world. We will serve others in the ways that Jesus served others. We will speak and act against injustice in the world. We will feed the hungry and find ways to change food policies. We will clothe the naked and minister to those who are homeless. We will visit those in prison and work to make the prison a place where individuals are restored to wholeness. We will make God's justice and love real on earth. We will find new ways to exercise stewardship for all creation. We will do all this because the world is worthy of redemption. God invites us to fast from apathy and to love the world as Jesus Christ loves the world.

For Your Growth

Day 1. Spend some time watching the local and national news or reading a newspaper. Make a list of the news stories—for example, international relations, national actions, concerns of the state, crime in the community. While the list may seem long, pray that you will recognize God's presence in these situations.

Day 2. Read the words of "What Wondrous Love Is This" again. Ask yourself why you believe that God thinks the world is worth redemption and love. Today, pray for each of the situations on the list you created on Day 1. Pray that God will bring reconciliation where division exists and justice where oppression rules.

Day 3. As you continue to ponder "What Wondrous Love Is This" and the gift of salvation, think about how God has transformed your life. Imagine what your neighborhood would look like with such a transformation. Is your neighborhood worth saving? Is your city or state worth redeeming? Invite God to inspire your imagination to see communities living fully in the reign of God. What does this look like to you?

Day 4. Take a look at your list of news stories again. Which stories seem less pressing or call for less attention? Which stories attract your interest and focus? What needs do you sense in these situations and circumstances? Begin to focus your prayers on these situations. Pray that God will show you how to use your gifts to minister to them. After you have finished praying, consider whether one story stands out over the others. Which seems to be calling for your attention the most? How might you show God's wondrous love in one of these situations?

The Next Day. Continue to pray for the situation(s) you started praying for on Day 4. After your prayer time, write the situation on a blank piece of paper and then begin to note all the ways you can help bring change and redemption to it. Consider this a time of personal brainstorming in which all ideas are good and none ridiculous. After ten minutes, evaluate your brainstorming list. Choose one of your solutions and move forward with it.

In the Days to Come. Pray the words of "What Wondrous Love Is This," and praise God for believing in the world and loving it. After your prayer time, take the first steps to move your solution from the previous day toward reality. Go on that visit. Make that telephone call. Send that e-mail. Write that letter. Talk to others at your church who may share a similar concern. Taking action is easier than living with the inertia of noncaring.

Questions for Further Consideration

1. What attitudes have you seen or experienced concerning fasting in general?
2. What did you learn about the spiritual aspects of apathy as you observed those attitudes?

3. What obstacles might you face in a fast from apathy?

4. What practices might help you avoid apathy toward life?

For Further Involvement

This short video from United Methodist TV features churches engaging in ministries of caring for others:

http://www.youtube.com/watch?v=bXs3ryeQ05Y

WEEK 2

Serving God by Serving Others

*Whoever wishes to be first among you must be
your slave; just as the Son of Man came not to
be served but to serve.*

—MATTHEW 20:27-28

MY FRIEND WHO GIVES UP liver for Lent is a potter. He volunteers in an after-school program for children who live in an urban neighborhood. Another friend, a musician, helps in a similar after-school program for children. Both programs offer safety and respite from life on the streets and a place to study and receive tutoring. Each program includes some basic Christian education and snacks (or meals) plus time to play and work off some of the energy the children have stored up during the day. These programs were started by church congregations that saw specific needs within their communities and began to work toward meeting those needs. The children do not participate in the congregations that engage in these ministries. They simply live in the same neighborhoods. The churches and those who help with these programs see their efforts as one way to serve those who live outside the community of faith.

If you have read Week 1 and started the exercises, you may be on your way toward fasting from apathy; however, I am not naïve enough to believe that any of us can change overnight (or even within a week). God's grace can do it, but we ourselves do not have that power. This book does not try to cure our apathy overnight but helps us move from internal practices of piety and devotion to external deeds of compassion and mercy.

The letter of James contains a sharp sentence that directly relates to what I am talking about here: "Do not merely listen to the word, and so deceive yourselves. Do what it says" (1:22, NIV). You may have encountered this thought before, or you may believe that preachers weave these words into every sermon. You would be right. Preachers often do weave these words into sermons. But if those sermons are like many that I have heard, they contain only generic suggestions about what to do. Often the sermons suggest that you follow the Bible's teachings and live by their meaning—or you are told to consider the plight of those who have less than you.

I ask you to consider a fresh approach to serving others and God. Perhaps more important, I suggest that you do what the Bible says. In the past twenty-five years or so, we have seen a great burst of interest in spirituality and the spiritual disciplines. Incredible numbers of books, lectures, and recordings on different aspects of prayer have become available. Prayer walks and prayer journals illustrate two distinctly different facets of prayer that are now popular. Private prayer and public prayer both figure as important practices in our Christian journey. Other individual practices include *lectio divina* (a formal approach to meditating on scripture), praying with icons, and praying while walking a labyrinth. Our communal practices of prayer include anointing with oil for healing, *Tongsung Kido* (the Korean practice in which all worshipers pray aloud at the same time), and the prayers of discipleship-accountability groups. These practices concern our inner life with God and help us to love God more deeply as we become open to God's direction in our daily lives.

We may notice that Jesus' early followers acted first and then began to observe spiritual practices like prayer and fasting. Sometimes that action was impetuous, like that of Peter when he cut off the ear of the high priest's slave in John 18. At other times, we see in scripture a balance between serving others through acts of compassion and serving God through acts of devotion. Our growing interior disciplines lead to external actions.

Prayers and Actions

After the Ascension, Jesus' followers gather in prayer to discern who will replace Judas among the Twelve (Acts 1:12-14). The disciples remain together until the festival of Pentecost. Notice the collective character and action of the disciples. Here we see the disciples in their first appearance independent of Jesus. Even though Jesus is no longer physically with his followers, they act in the way Jesus did before any major decision: They spend time in prayer.

At the festival of Pentecost, the disciples receive the Holy Spirit in amazing ways, and the Spirit prompts them to communicate in other languages so that the Jews around them can understand. In Acts 2 we see prayer undergirding the disciples' first acts of ministry. We witness initial results of this ministry. Throughout the book of Acts, the ministry of the disciples develops through acts of service and witness. The disciples' lives offer models of prayer and service.

An Interruption

Let's be clear about the origin of Pentecost. Pentecost is the Greek name for *shavu'ot*, the Jewish Feast of Weeks or Festival of Reaping. *Shavu'ot*, the Feast of Weeks, was one of the three pilgrimage festivals for Jews. (Passover and the Feast of Booths are the other two.) The Feast of Weeks was a one-day festival that celebrated the first fruits of the wheat harvest. The time to celebrate the Feast of Weeks came the fiftieth day after the offering of the barley sheaf at the Feast of Unleavened Bread, which is part of the Passover observance. Because *shavu'ot* occurs fifty days after Passover, Jews during the Hellenistic period began calling it Pentecost. Now back to the story.

On the day of Pentecost the disciples communicate the gospel in a multitude of languages. The list of languages covers the civilized world known to most first-century followers of Jesus. In Acts 2 Peter addresses the crowds who have gathered around the disciples—in part, because these followers of

Jesus are speaking in languages that they did not know five minutes earlier. Peter speaks so boldly about Jesus Christ that the people ask, "What should we do?" (Acts 2:37). Peter does not extend an altar call; the people invite themselves to the invisible altar of grace. People are baptized and then devote themselves to apostolic teaching and fellowship, the breaking of bread, and prayer (Acts 2:42).

Notice how the disciples' prayers led to Christian witness and holy conversation on the day of Pentecost. I could argue against myself and say that the disciples did not choose to act but were moved to do so by the Holy Spirit. I believe, however, that the prayers of the disciples prior to the event prepared and opened the way for them to receive the Holy Spirit. Had the disciples not engaged in prayer throughout the time following Jesus' ascension, would the Holy Spirit have appeared in such a dramatic way on the day of Pentecost? Had the disciples not engaged in prayer, would they have recognized the Holy Spirit's presence when it arrived? Thank God the disciples engaged in the practices of prayer, receptivity, and discernment!

The Bible does not teach prayer methods. When we read biblical stories about prayer, we find that someone has gone apart or has gone to be alone. We see powerful stories of prayer such as that of Jacob wrestling with the angel at Peniel and Jesus in the garden at Gethsemane. We see other times when the Bible only hints at prayer. In John 21 Peter declares, "I'm going fishing." For Peter, that act of fishing may also become prayer.

I tend to be an introvert. Sitting in silence and contemplating the mystery of God's love is part of my daily practice.

I have an extroverted friend, also a United Methodist pastor, who was struggling with his vocational call and with his congregation. As we talked, he said, "I am not finding God in what I do on Sunday morning or in my connections with people." I asked about his prayer life, and he brushed away the question. I suggested he spend five minutes in silent meditation upon Mark 1:16-20, the calling of the first disciples by Jesus. "You don't understand me," Tom said. "I can't be silent for a minute without feeling ill. I've tried. When I have, it felt as if the silence were chaos pushing against everything in me. I'll never hear God in that." So we talked further, and I suggested that he begin spending more time at the homeless shelter in his community. He did, and over the next months he received a renewed sense of vocation. Our personalities help shape our prayers. For more about personality and prayer, see the Postscript at the end of this book.

Serving Others

The letter of James contains advice for Christian service and witness. The letter was circulated to churches made up of both Jewish and Gentile Christians who may have misunderstood and were misapplying Paul's teachings on faith and the nature of love. Paul's message focuses on salvation through faith and not by works. Some of the early Christians interpret Paul to mean that Christians need not serve or minister to others. They fear contamination by the world and demonstrate an unwillingness to engage the world in ministry or mission. They consider their faith to be something that can be lost or stolen, so they try to protect it.

James's letter offers vital witness to the fact that we gain strength in our faith and discipleship by serving others. Instead of a pure faith that avoids contamination from the world, the letter states the following: "Religion that God our Father accepts as pure and faultless is this: to look after orphans and widows in their distress and to keep oneself from being polluted by the world" (James 1:27, NIV). James 2:14 reveals more about the situation being addressed: "What good is it, my brothers and sisters, if you say you have faith but do not have works?" These verses and others offer a corrective to a perspective that will not allow Christian faith to be soiled or contaminated by the difficulties presented by the world. We do not have the luxury to choose *either* faith *or* works. Christian discipleship calls us to live by faith *and* to demonstrate that faith through our works.

In seventeenth-century France, a monk named Brother Lawrence emphasized the practice of prayer in the midst of all our activities. In the monastery, Brother Lawrence scrubbed pots, did errands for others, and baked bread. He prayed for the other monks as he made, shaped, and baked each loaf. He prayed while planting seeds and weeding vegetable patches and as he went about his other daily activities.

> We search for stated ways and methods of learning how to love GOD, and to come at that love we disquiet our minds by I know not how many devices; we give ourselves a world of trouble and pursue a multitude of practices to attain to a sense of the Presence of God. And yet it is so simple. How very much shorter it is and easier to do our *common business* purely *for the love of God.*

Practicing the presence of God in all activities became Brother Lawrence's priority. He affirmed the wisdom of the apostle Paul: "We have this treasure in clay jars" (2 Cor. 4:7). We are all ordinary people, but the extraordinary love of God resides within us. How do we instill within us that greater awareness of God's love and grace? Brother Lawrence offers this approach:

> We can do *little* things for God; I turn the cake that is frying on the pan for love of Him, and that done, if there is nothing else to call me, I prostrate myself in worship before Him, Who has given me grace to work; afterwards I rise happier than a king. It is enough for me to pick up but a straw from the ground for the love of God.[3]

Practicing the presence of God in all activities was not an easy habit for Brother Lawrence, and such a discipline does not come easily to us. Yet as we undertake our daily tasks, we can begin to associate them with God's grace. Whether we are taking out the trash or telephoning a local official about political change or knocking on doors with a petition or cooking a meal to feed the homeless, we are reminded of God's love in the midst of our engagement. Brother Lawrence says about his work in the monastery kitchen:

> The time of business does not with me differ from the time of prayer; and in the noise and clatter of my kitchen, while several persons are at the same time calling for different things, I possess GOD in as great tranquility as if I were upon my knees at the blessed sacrament.[4]

As we serve others, we show our love for God. Our service is a form of prayer and devotion. When we pray for God to show love to all the world, we promise to show God's love to the world through *our* actions.

A Charge to Keep I Have

John Wesley described Methodism's purpose as a movement in this way: to "reform the nation and, in particular, the Church; to spread scriptural holiness over the land." The Wesley brothers came to this perspective after much Bible study and prayer. In eighteenth-century England, the Church of England was the national church. The Wesleys felt, however, that it did not speak to the needs of the people or address the social ills within the nation at the time. The Wesleyan understanding of mission took shape during this era as John and Charles addressed social needs like education, poverty, disease, and mental health in their preaching and teaching.

Methodist Christians began the first Sunday schools to teach children how to read. They collected offerings to alleviate the conditions of those in poverty. In a time when medical doctors were concentrated in London, Methodist circuit preachers carried copies of *Primitive Physick* with them, a book by John Wesley that helped diagnose and apply medical techniques to those who were ill.

Methodists also worked to change the appalling conditions in mental institutions and jails. By proclaiming the grace of Jesus Christ, the Wesleys brought change to many of the social ills in England. Persisting in this mission remained a challenge in the lifetime of the Wesleys. John was not always welcomed in places where he preached and ministered. Other Methodists faced contempt and ridicule.

James Logan, in *How Great a Flame*, tells the story of Martha Thompson, a housemaid in London born in 1731. While doing errands she passed a crowd of people who were singing outdoors. She listened to the singing and then noticed a small man who began preaching to the crowd. It was John Wesley. When she returned home and told her mistress what she saw, the mistress told her to avoid Wesley because "he will drive you mad, he will ruin you."

Martha, however, returned often to hear John Wesley preach. One day during the singing of "The Lord Jehovah Reigns," she experienced an inner peace, which Wesley called the "inner witness of the Spirit." She continued to praise and give glory to God, even after she had returned home. Ultimately, this led to her committal at Bedlam, a notorious mental asylum. At Bedlam she continued to witness for Christ. Thompson was eventually released from Bedlam and remained an active Methodist Christian witness until her death.

Stories similar to Martha Thompson's were common in eighteenth-century England. Methodists were often unwelcome in society, and their words and actions brought hostility. Charles Wesley, inspired by his reading of Matthew Henry's commentary on Leviticus 8:35, wrote a hymn of encouragement to the early Methodists who were experiencing animosity from the public.

> A charge to keep I have,
> a God to glorify,
> a never-dying soul to save,
> and fit it for the sky.

To serve the present age,
my calling to fulfill;
O may it all my powers engage
to do my Master's will!

Arm me with jealous care,
as in thy sight to live,
and oh, thy servant, Lord, prepare
a strict account to give!

Help me to watch and pray,
and on thyself rely,
assured, if I my trust betray,
I shall forever die.

This hymn offers strength and comfort to Christians of the eighteenth- and twenty-first centuries alike, all of whom have received as their calling to fulfill, "to serve the present age." The hymn speaks to all aspects of Christian ministry and mission. Whenever we sing this hymn, we reaffirm the call of Christ to engage in ministry with the world.

O may it all my powers engage
to do my Master's will!

We may pay no attention to the meaning of these words as we sing them, but they speak of our common ties with Christians around the world to bear witness to grace through word and deed.

We find one of the clearest statements of God's will in Matthew 25:31-46 where Jesus speaks about the judgment of the nations. Jesus says to those at his right hand:

> Come, you that are blessed by my Father,
> inherit the kingdom prepared for you from the

> foundation of the world; for I was hungry and
> you gave me food, I was thirsty and you gave
> me something to drink, I was a stranger and you
> welcomed me, I was naked and you gave me
> clothing, I was sick and you took care of me, I
> was in prison and you visited me" (vv. 34-36).

These words express the actions that Christ wills for us. Not only are these actions a charge we have been given, they are a charge we have to keep. God invites us to find deep satisfaction in the work.

For Your Growth

Day 1. Continue to watch the local and national news programs or read a print or online newspaper. Make a list of news stories—for example, international relations, national actions, concerns of the state, crime in the community. While the list may seem long, pray that God's presence will be revealed in these situations.

Day 2. Read the words of "A Charge to Keep I Have" again. Consider why you believe that God thinks the world is worthy of redemption and love. Today, pray for each of the situations on the list you created the day before. Pray that God will bring reconciliation where division exists and justice where oppression rules.

Day 3. Think about the story of Martha Thompson and her mistress's response to Wesley: "He will drive you mad, he will ruin you." Martha spent time in an asylum because of her faith in Christ. Where will your faith in Christ take you? In what surprising or unexpected place will you engage in ministry?

Day 4. In what ways has God transformed your life? Imagine what your neighborhood would look like if it were to experience a similar transformation. Is your neighborhood worth saving? What would a transformed neighborhood begin to look like? What changes do you imagine would take place first? Invite God to inspire your imagination to see communities living fully in the reign of God.

The Next Day. Continue to pray for the news story or report that has held your attention this week. Ask God what you can do about the situation. After your prayer time, write the situation on a blank piece of paper and begin to note all the ways you can help bring change and redemption to it. Consider this a time of personal brainstorming in which all ideas are good, and none is ridiculous.

After ten or fifteen minutes, evaluate the brainstorming list. Choose one solution, and move forward with it.

In the Days to Come. Pray the words of "A Charge to Keep I Have," and praise God for believing in the world and loving it. After your prayer time, take the first steps to move your solution toward reality. Go on that visit. Make that telephone call. Send that e-mail. Write that letter. Talk to others at your church who may share a similar concern. Taking action is easier than living with the inertia of noncaring.

Questions for Further Consideration

1. What does it mean to serve God by serving others?

2. What new opportunities to serve God do you see in your community?

3. After reading and praying "A Charge to Keep I Have," how do you understand your charge? Where is God leading you?

4. When others respond that your dream for serving others is not realistic, what will you do to show them that it is?

For Further Involvement

Inside the Box Café in Tampa, Florida, serves a variety of needs in mission. Here is a short video about the café from United Methodist TV:

http://www.youtube.com/watch?v=dQ5Ree4YMlY

WEEK 3

Feeding Others and Starving Our Guilt

*I was hungry and you gave me food, I was
thirsty and you gave me something to drink.*
—MATTHEW 25:35

I AM AN AMERICAN of Armenian descent. My mother and
father were first-generation Armenian-Americans. My grandparents managed to escape the genocide of 1915 in the Otto-
man Empire. My father's two older brothers did not survive
the genocide. While my parents tried to avoid telling me
about the genocide, whenever we went to Armenian Church
services and festivals, we heard survivor stories. In adolescence and adulthood, I learned from outside the family about
the genocide of at least one million Armenians and the effort
to destroy all signs of the Armenian culture within the Otto-
man Empire. Many acquaintances, coworkers, and friends
first learned about the genocide from my mini-lectures.

One of my friends owns a memorabilia business that sells art and print ads from old magazines. Imagine my surprise when I opened a gift from her and found an ad from a 1920 issue of *The Saturday Evening Post*. The full-page ad contains a heartbreaking photo of a sad-eyed Armenian child. The advertising copy, sponsored by Buster Brown Shoes, a company that made shoes for children, reads as follows:

> This Little Armenian Is Appealing to YOU
> He is the son of an Armenian shoemaker.
> Look into his sweet pathetic eyes. He is well
> and strong now. But in his eyes you still can
> read something of the frightful agony that is
> overwhelming the Near East. For three years
> he tramped the war-swept lands. When the
> American Relief Workers found him, crying for
> the loving arms that could no longer rock him
> to sleep, his only garment was a strip of rag, the
> relic of his shirt.

The ad continued its appeal to a collective sense of guilt. It ends with these words:

> They are relying on YOU. Do your share.
> Never was there a worthier cause. These people,
> held down for centuries by Turkish oppression,
> are bright and industrious. Once started anew,
> they will quickly establish themselves. What is
> given now they will repay a hundredfold. Open
> your heart. Open your pocketbook.

I do not know the results of that advertising campaign. Some older friends told me that as children their parents urged them to eat their carrots because the starving Armenians had none. I do know that similar descriptive efforts were used to help the Armenians experiencing genocide in Azerbaijan in 1988. Based on the number of people who have not heard about the 1915 massacre, an event that gave rise to the coining of the word *genocide* by Raphael Lemkin, these ads did little for the general awareness and collective memory of the public.

Most Americans have not experienced genocide or the horrors of massive starvation firsthand. We have seen pictures and news reports from places like Biafra, Cambodia, Uganda, Serbia, Rwanda, and Syria. We see these stories and try to block from our memory the horror of lives destroyed. Charitable organizations appeal to us for money for relief efforts in various countries. These appeals for charitable aid have not changed much since the 1920 Buster Brown ad. Charities and foundations continue appeals to induce us to feel guilt and persuade us to give. Because we anticipate efforts to induce guilt, we toss that well-crafted appeal letter into the recycling bin or forward our way through the commercial to avoid feelings of guilt.

Guilt is a lousy way to gain support even for the most worthy cause. It may persuade us to give some of our money, but giving money only does good in the *short term*. Guilt does little to connect us with the deeper needs and causes of these situations. It does not necessarily encourage us to take action that will effect change.

In Week 1 I referred to compassion fatigue and in Week 2 to Jesus' parable about the judgment of the nations in Matthew 25. I invite you to think more deeply about this parable and the reasons for Jesus' telling it.

Before we consider the parable, think with me a bit about compassion fatigue or burnout. Those in vocations that involve caring for others are prone to such compassion fatigue, especially when dealing with periods of extended caregiving without respite. Such times may produce a combination of physical and mental and emotional exhaustion. Continuing education units address compassion fatigue for those in the field of healthcare, especially nurses. Clergy receive cautions about spiritual burnout, which seems to me to be a form of compassion fatigue. We are all busy people, but the majority of us are not facing situations of extended caregiving. When Jesus offered the parable recorded in Matthew 25:31-46, he addressed ordinary people; he invited them to engage in his mission and ministry. I believe that Jesus intended this parable as good news.

Jesus Heals the Broken

When Jesus addressed people's needs, he did not condemn them. He brought healing—physical, mental, emotional, and spiritual. He received and accepted those considered ritually unclean by the culture and the Law. Imagine this scene from John 8: It is early morning in the Temple courtyard. Many people have come to hear Jesus teach about God. Suddenly a group of Pharisees and scribes show up with a woman they have caught in the act of adultery. She may have been naked if caught in the act, and the Pharisees knew that her nakedness would humiliate her and her family even more. No reference is made to her sexual partner, only that the Pharisees had caught the woman in the act. Deuteronomy

22 calls for the death of those caught in adultery—both parties—in order to "purge the evil from Israel" (v. 22). But the scribes and Pharisees bring only the woman. "Now in the law Moses commanded us to stone such women. Now what do you say?" the Pharisees ask Jesus (John 8:5). Jesus is silent at first. He writes on the ground of the courtyard while the Pharisees and scribes continue questioning him. Finally, Jesus straightens up and says, "Let anyone among you who is without sin be the first to throw a stone at her" (John 8:7). Then Jesus kneels again and continues to write in the ground. The scribes, Pharisees, and bystanders leave. Only Jesus and the woman remain. Jesus asks her, "Where are they? Has no one condemned you?" (John 8:10). "No one, sir," she replies (John 8:11). "Neither do I condemn you. Go your way, and from now on do not sin again" (John 8:11).

The woman and her partner are guilty of breaking the law, yet Jesus offers her forgiveness and grace. As I imagine the life of this unnamed woman, I envision her telling others about the new life she has received from Jesus. She is like the Samaritan woman who told her friends and neighbors about Jesus, "Come and see a man who told me everything I have ever done! He cannot be the Messiah, can he?" (John 4:29). For Jesus, guilt is not part of the equation. Grace, forgiveness, and joy are the formula.

I tell this story to remind us that Jesus does not inflict guilt; he takes away sin and guilt. Even when Jesus accuses the establishment of laying heavy burdens on the people or at other times when he acts with a sense of God's justice, I do not think that Jesus attempted to induce guilt. The parties may have felt guilty after the confrontation, but Jesus' actions always sought to break class and cultural bondage. He heals our broken nature and removes barriers that cause us to live less than whole lives. As I read the Gospels, I see Jesus offering wholeness of life—another way to think about salvation—to people who have been broken because of their own actions or those of the larger culture or government. Nowhere does Jesus *create* a guilt trip for anyone.

In Matthew 25 Jesus says of those who will be blessed by his Father, "for I was hungry and you gave me food, I was thirsty and you gave me something to drink, I was a stranger and you welcomed me, I was naked and you gave me clothing, I was sick and you took care of me, I was in prison and you visited me" (vv. 35-36).

Notice what Jesus actually says in this parable. The parable consists of two surprises. The first surprise concerns those who Jesus says are "blessed by my Father" (v. 34). The second surprise occurs when those Jesus calls righteous ask when they did these things, and Jesus responds, "Just as you did it to one of the least of these who are members of my family, you did it to me" (v. 40).

People often use the text of Matthew 25:31-46 to inflict guilt. Too many sermons and Bible studies have beaten this passage into the shape of a sword. Worse, many people have employed its words to encourage service to others—heavy-handed appeals similar to the 1920 ad to raise funds for Armenians after the genocide.

Jesus' words in Matthew 25 are neither angry nor are they efforts to induce guilt. Jesus makes observations about his followers. He speaks of blessings because they have acted selflessly in serving others. In the Gospels, Jesus speaks of the greatest disciples as becoming the lowest. (See Mark 8:31-36.) He tells his followers to serve, even to give a cup of cold water to children. (See Matt. 10:40-42.) He does not inflict guilt; he simply reminds them to give as God gives and to serve as he serves. Jesus embodies servant-leadership, and he invites his followers to do so as well.

On the other side of the parable of the judgment in Matthew 25, Jesus recognizes the lack of compassionate action from those at his left hand. I sense sadness more than anger in his words: "Depart from me . . . for I was hungry and you gave me no food, I was thirsty and you gave me nothing to drink, I was a stranger and you did not welcome me, naked and you did not give me clothing, sick and in prison and you did not visit me" (Matt. 25:41-43).

Those to whom Jesus speaks ask when they did *not* do these things (v. 44). His answer presents a call to action: "Just as you did not do it to one of the least of these, you did not do it to me" (v. 45). Either by action or inaction, these people have made themselves guilty. Jesus does not instill guilt within us. He offers healing.

Guilt comes to many of us through the power of advertising that implies if we are good parents we will buy the latest nutritional and conveniently packaged food for our children (with the implicit message that if we do *not* buy it, we are guilty of bad parenting). The voice of guilt speaks when we fail to buy the newest clothing or latest electronic equipment or to take our families on a vacation cruise. Guilt comes as it sets in opposition those who have and those who have not.

Jesus invites people to follow him and to live in God's reign. Our response to God's call reorients our priorities. We feel less concerned about the things we may get and more concerned about what we offer and give to others. Because Christ transforms our lives, our priorities shift. We focus on God's expectation that we show mercy and justice for all creation. Jesus teaches us about God's love and calls us to reorient our lives in love of God and neighbor. He calls us to live compassionately—in service to those in need. Then we have little need to listen to the voice of guilt. Our compassionate love for others starves our guilt.

Feeding Others

When you observe news reports during the week, notice stories about hunger in the United States or around the world. How do you respond to these stories? Do you think, *I've seen enough?* What feelings do these stories generate? What actions do you take? What do you hear God saying to you as you pray?

In 1978 three couples—the Reverend Ken and Jean Horne, the Reverend Ray and Marian Buchanan, and the Reverend Jeff and Susan Allen—began praying daily for God's guidance in beginning a shared ministry: an intentional Christian community to focus on the problem of world hunger. One year later they presented their plan to Bishop W. Kenneth Goodson of the Virginia Annual Conference of The United Methodist Church. That year Bishop Goodson appointed Ken Horne and Ray Buchanan to form the Society of Saint Andrew, a ministry to deal with world hunger. While leading a workshop on Virginia's Eastern Shore, an area in which farming is the principal occupation, a local farmer challenged Horne and Buchanan. He had sweet potatoes that were too large, too small, or misshapen. They were unacceptable to commercial buyers but still edible. A discussion followed, and the conversation led to the birth of the Potato and Produce Project. On June 3, 1983, the Society of Saint Andrew received its first tractor-trailer load of sweet potatoes, which were then delivered to the Central Virginia Food Bank in Richmond.

Two years later, in 1985, the Society of Saint Andrew began Harvest of Hope, a study and gleaning camp for youth. The youth learned about the problems of world hunger as they gleaned in the fields. Like Ruth, who is the best-known biblical gleaner, these youth salvaged edible tomatoes, potatoes, and other vegetables that had no commercial viability (often because they were not aesthetically pleasing). Over the years, the Society of Saint Andrew has donated more than five hundred million pounds of food to hungry people in the United States. The Society has grown beyond the dream of those first three couples and now has regional offices in the United States.

Ray Buchanan left the Society of Saint Andrew to begin a new ministry called Stop Hunger Now, an international hunger relief agency formed in 1998 with a commitment to end world hunger. Based in Raleigh, North Carolina, Stop Hunger Now coordinates the distribution of food and other lifesaving aid to people around the world. Their mission statement: "To end hunger in our lifetime by providing food and life-saving aid to the world's most vulnerable and by creating a global commitment to mobilize the necessary resources."

Many churches participate in a meal-packaging program begun in 2005 by Stop Hunger Now. The program combines rice, soy, dehydrated vegetables, and a flavoring mix including twenty-one essential vitamins and minerals into small meal packets and distributes these packets through school feeding programs in hunger-stricken regions.

I invite you to consider these two ministries to end hunger in our world. They began with the inner discipline of prayer. *What would you have us do in intentional ministry? What would you have us do for the least of these?* God's response came in a gradually unfolding process. A vision of dealing with world hunger came first, followed by the formation of an intentional community to teach about the problems of hunger. From the workshops and teaching moments came the gleaning project and efforts to end hunger within the United States. From that emerged the ministry of Stop Hunger Now, an effort to end global hunger. I heard Ray Buchanan speak at a church that I pastored. He offered words of gracious invitation to join him and others in fighting hunger. His positive message showed no pictures of starving children—Armenian or otherwise. He simply talked about making the love of Jesus Christ visible to others through our actions.

Another way we can feed others involves looking at our cities and the patterns of food distribution within the urban core. Mark Winne in *Closing the Food Gap* describes food deserts—areas in low-income neighborhoods where supermarkets either charge higher prices or have gone out of business leaving residents to depend on convenience stores for food needs. Having lived in one such urban area for twenty years, I saw the price gouging. I engaged store managers in conversation about the higher prices. I heard management stories of theft and loss and, as one who grew up in a corner grocery store, I understood the concerns of managers. While my neighborhood could not help the store owners, the member of my congregation responded to the hunger in the area by feeding children in the after-school program, packing knapsacks with food for distribution at the neighborhood elementary school on the last Friday of the month, teaching nutrition and economic education through after-school and parenting classes, and beginning a community garden. These changes, while small in scale, offered us opportunities to feed others.

Love Divine, All Loves Excelling

One of the most loved Wesleyan hymns is "Love Divine, All Loves Excelling." The British royalty even used the hymn at a wedding. In more ordinary times and places, we sing this hymn often.

The hymn contains four stanzas that offer a trinitarian understanding of God. The first stanza speaks of Jesus Christ, the incarnate redeemer of the world:

Love divine, all loves excelling,
joy of heaven, to earth come down;
fix in us thy humble dwelling;
all thy faithful mercies crown!
Jesus, thou art all compassion,
pure, unbounded love thou art;
visit us with thy salvation;
enter every trembling heart.

The second stanza focuses on the Holy Spirit and its gifts. Stanza three speaks of God as the one source of all life.

The final stanza points us in a slightly different direction and speaks of a culmination of history and the transformation of the old order into the new:

Finish, then, thy new creation;
pure and spotless let us be.
Let us see thy great salvation
perfectly restored in thee;
changed from glory into glory,
till in heaven we take our place,
till we cast our crowns before thee,
lost in wonder, love, and praise.

The words of the hymn point us to an understanding of God's radical love for the world. I sometimes wonder if we pay attention to what we sing. Wesley's hymn is rich with biblical references: "'I am the Alpha and the Omega'" (Rev. 21:6); "they cast their crowns before the throne, singing" (Rev. 4:10); "transformed . . . from one degree of glory to another" (2 Cor. 3:18).

God indeed believes the world is worth redeeming; hence, the incarnation of Jesus Christ, Son of God, savior of the world. To me, this Wesley hymn indicates the redemptive work of God in the world and issues an invitation to engage with God in its ongoing transformation.

The new creation is a common theme in the Bible and often spoken of in terms of hope. In Isaiah we read, "For I am about to create new heavens and a new earth; / the former things shall not be remembered or come to mind" (65:17). We read in Second Peter: "But, in accordance with his promise, we wait for new heavens and a new earth, where righteousness is at home" (3:13). In Revelation, we find these words: "I saw a new heaven and a new earth; for the first heaven and the first earth had passed away" (21:1). The book of Revelation speaks a word of hope about God's ultimate victory and the rebirth of all the earth. The day is coming, say the prophets and biblical writers, when God will wipe away our tears and comfort us. In that day God will feed all of us and care for our needs. Until then, Christ invites us to join him in feeding the hungry of the world, working toward the completion of the new creation, and becoming changed ourselves—from glory into glory and from this life into a new one.

Singing hymns of praise to God—engaging in the spiritual discipline of worship—always leads to service in the world that God created and is redeeming.

For Your Growth

Day 1. Find out what food and feeding programs exist in your community. Some suggestions: Ask your pastor. If your community has a library, talk to the librarian about what he or she sees with regard to hunger and homelessness. Telephone the local social services agency, and ask what can be done to help with hunger in the area. Call the local government—mayor, city council, and/or county supervisors—and ask if food is provided to those who are hungry and how that food is delivered. How can you help feed hungry people through these community channels?

Day 2. What have you learned about food banks in your area? Does your church provide food to those in need? If so, does it give nonperishable food on a regular basis or during emergency? Does your church have a feeding program, like a breakfast ministry? What churches in the area support feeding programs or community Meals on Wheels programs?

Day 3. How can you engage in existing ministries that feed people? Can you volunteer on a weekly basis? collect food or money? publicize and promote needs?

Day 4. What feelings have you noticed within yourself as you learn about the problems of hunger and about the response of church or community to these needs? Do you find yourself responding with a greater sense of God's justice for all people, or do you sense some remnants of guilt? Take time to pray about your motivation for this ministry.

The Next Day. How would you publicize or promote hunger ministries? Would you create a radio ad? a web page? signs? Who would you tell about such ministries?

In the Days to Come. As you feed others, engage in conversation about spirituality. Listen, learn, teach, and pray. The next time you sing "Love Divine, All Loves Excelling" in church, enjoy the gift of the joy of heaven to earth come down!

Questions for Further Consideration

1. What have you learned from this week's reading about guilt as a way of eliciting support?
2. How did Jesus involve people in his mission?
3. Who and where are the hungry people in your area?
4. What steps will you take—as an individual, a small-group participant, a congregation—to deal with hunger?

For Further Involvement

Learn more about food deserts by reading *Closing the Food Gap: Resetting the Table in the Land of Plenty,* by Mark Winne (Beacon Press, 2008).

Contact information for the Society of Saint Andrew
sosausa@endhunger.org
3383 Sweet Hollow Road
Big Island, Virginia 24526
800-333-4597
www.endhunger.org

Stop Hunger Now: info@stophungernow.org
615 Hillsborough St., Suite 200, Raleigh, North Carolina 27603
Toll Free: 888-501-8440
You can also find a list of regional offices on the website: www.stophungernow.org

Bread for the World, a Christian group, deals with hunger by lobbying our nation's leaders to end hunger within the United States and around the world. Learn more on its

website: www.bread.org
   425 3rd Street SW
   Suite 1200
   Washington, DC 20024
   800-822-7323

A brief video that concerns urban food deserts.

   http://www.youtube.com/watch?v=t2w5RrGPD1Q

Another video that features gleaning and the Society of Saint Andrew.

   http://www.youtube.com/watch?v=vwF4jXA_CuE

WEEK 4

Seeking Justice

Happy are those
who do not follow the advice
of the wicked.

—Psalm 1:1

The prophet Amos speaks of justice flowing down like a stream
(see Amos 5:24). The book of Micah records these words:

[God] has told you, O mortal, what is good;
and what does the Lord require of you
but to do justice, and to love kindness,
and to walk humbly with your God? (6:8).

Writing about the faithlessness of Israel, the prophet
Hosea makes the following statement:

But as for you, return to your God,
hold fast to love and justice,
and wait continually for your God (12:6).

The prophet Isaiah says,

> Learn to do good;
> seek justice,
>   rescue the oppressed,
> defend the orphan,
>   plead for the widow (1:17).

How do we define justice? Many people think about justice as our system of crime and punishment. When I ask people what justice means, they say, "Justice is what you get when you do wrong" or "Justice is not as strict as it used to be in this country" and "The courts need to look more seriously at prison sentences to make the punishment fit the crime." They identify aspects of the judicial system. While our courts and prisons serve the cause of justice, the prophets Isaiah, Micah, and Amos had a larger plan in mind.

Nearly eighteen hundred years before the birth of Jesus, the Babylonian king Hammurabi created the first known set of written laws to govern everyday life. The laws were specific and covered business and trade, military service, duties of workers, slavery, and religion. The basic principle behind Hammurabi's code is known as *lex talionis*. Law 196 offers a basic example of *lex talionis*: "If a man put out the eye of another man, his eye shall be put out." In Hammurabi's code the punishment fit the crime.

Our legal codes have expanded since the day of Hammurabi. Many laws remain based on the principle of *lex talionis*. These examples demonstrate a specific effort to seek justice known as retributive justice. Retributive justice seeks to regulate our response to legally proven crime so that the culture considers the punishment morally right and fully deserved by the criminal. Once upon a time, people hoped that prisons could change lives and provide rehabilitation through education and training, but rehabilitation no longer takes place because of a variety of factors that include overcrowding and underfunding.

The concern of restorative justice, on the other hand, focuses on making the victim whole and returning the offender to society. Those who advocate a restorative approach often bring offender and victim together so the offender can understand the effect his or her offense has had on the victim. Restorative justice provided the basis for the Truth and Reconciliation Commission in South Africa after the end of legal racial segregation known as apartheid. During the Commission's hearings, individuals who were identified as having been severely violated were invited to face those who had perpetrated the abuse and to testify to their experience.

Recall the words of the prophets about justice. Are the prophets speaking about retributive or restorative justice?

Think about justice in terms of the following questions:

- Do we call it *justice* when we feed people who are hungry? Or when we clothe those in need?

- Is justice visiting people who are in prison? Is it justice when we do good deeds for others?

- Do we advance the cause of justice when we collect clothing for those whose lives have been disrupted by natural disasters or when we put together a team of volunteers to do cleanup or construction work in an area destroyed by a hurricane or tornado?

These actions are deeds of mercy that show compassion for others and are directed toward individuals. These actions contain the seeds of justice. Seeking justice means we work for what God intends for the world. We seek God's dream of wholeness for individuals and nations, and we work to establish systems in which all people receive equitable treatment and where oppression no longer rules.

Justice in the Bible

Our difficulty in defining justice (other than the criminal system) creates a difficulty in our implementing justice—putting justice into action. We turn to the Bible for guidance. Isaiah 1:17 offers direction for finding justice and, perhaps more importantly, discovering injustice. Earlier in Isaiah, the prophet speaks for God who calls the people a "sinful nation" (1:4). Isaiah then states, "What to me is the multitude of your sacrifices? says the LORD; I have had enough of burnt offerings of rams" (v. 11).

After these words comes instruction to "learn to do good; seek justice, rescue the oppressed, defend the orphan, plead for the widow" (v. 17). Each of these actions is a step toward justice. But we need to go deeper into the words of the prophet and into our biblical foundation if we are to understand truly what justice means.

God's call to action comes to the entire nation, not to one individual. The biblical understanding of justice involves the entire community or nation. The Bible does not know a solitary or individual faith when it comes to justice. Even when an individual receives instructions from God, as Abram did in Genesis 12, the response always involves others—Abram, Sarai, Lot, "and the persons whom they had acquired in Haran" (v. 5).

Many of us today think of faith as an individual matter. We think about individual rights and responsibilities and about the faith of individuals. When we extend invitations to discipleship in worship, those invitations are often calls to commit oneself to Christ. Sometimes we elevate the individual Christian to a place of importance higher than the community of faith itself. We so readily see the individual Christian that we lose sight of the body of Christ—the Christian community. Our sense of Christian individualism comes from a marriage between the Protestant Reformation idea of *sola fide* ("by faith alone") and the principles of the Enlightenment, which stressed the importance of individual reason over tradition, revelation, and faith. If we join the Enlightenment idea of individual reason and Protestantism's principle of *sola fide,* we end up with individuals who meditate by the sea without demonstrating signs of Christian belief to those around them.

I know Christians who live in other nations: Protestants, Catholics, and Orthodox Christians. They express concern for the whole Christian community and for ways in which the church can season its nations with the salt of discipleship. They share meals with one another and with those in need. They speak out against injustice. Friends in South Africa have experienced jail and prison time because of their beliefs and their advocacy for God's justice. Christian friends in Iran and Iraq have survived beatings and other abuses because of their beliefs and actions. Many have not survived the abuses they have suffered. My friends have been able to speak out against injustice in their societies because of their security in Christ.

Behind God's call to do good and seek justice—whether the words come from Isaiah or Micah or Jesus—is God's dream for the world. We first glimpse God's dream for the world in the Creation story in Genesis 1 when God saw that it was good. We see more of God's dream for the world in Isaiah 11, a passage often identified with the season of Advent and the coming of Christ, when the prophet speaks of the shoot that shall come from the family of Jesse:

> The wolf shall live with the lamb,
>> the leopard shall lie down with the kid,
> The calf and the lion and the fatling together,
>> and a little child shall lead them.
> . . . .
> The nursing child shall play over the hole of the asp,
>> and the weaned child shall put its hand
>> on the adder's den.
> They will not hurt or destroy
>> on all my holy mountain;
> for the earth will be full of the knowledge of the LORD
> as the waters cover the sea (vv. 6, 8-9).

The key to God's dream of justice is that no one will hurt or destroy anyone or anything—individuals, nations, and the earth itself. We will grow more deeply into God's love in such a way that the earth will be filled with the knowledge of God. War, famine, and violence tarnish that dream on many levels. When one group of people oppresses another group, God's dream fades. When orphans are forced to rear themselves and their younger siblings because their parents have died in war or from HIV-AIDS, God's dream suffers. When widows become the prey of those filled with greed, God's dream disappears. God invites us to do good by seeking justice, rescuing the oppressed, defending the orphan, and pleading for the widow. God's invitation is for the entire community and the nation.

Our understanding of these appropriate actions brings us to a place where we might begin to fathom justice. Justice addresses systems that oppress people or any portion of God's creation. When we help a homeless widow or military veteran, we are offering mercy. When we feed a meal to a hungry person, we offer mercy. When our church establishes a program that feeds people 365 days a year, we offer mercy. When we become involved with a group such as Bread for the World, then we begin addressing the systemic causes of hunger and working for justice.

God's Dream for the World

When we see news stories and talk to the people around us, we start to get a sense of the world's brokenness. We see stories of warfare and oppression, hunger in the midst of plenty, lack of medical care, prostitution, and slavery. This is not what God dreams for the world. God dreams of a kingdom in which the wolf and the lamb, the child and the poisonous snake, the Democrat and the Republican come together under one peaceable kingdom.

In God's dream, people use their gifts to care for all creation. No one will have dominion; all will be stewards. Such a vision offers us a new understanding of justice and our role in bringing it to the world. Individuals alone cannot change the destructive systems and powers of the world. As communities of faithful disciples, God works through us to bring change.

In *Letter from Birmingham Jail*, Martin Luther King Jr. wrote, "Injustice anywhere is a threat to justice everywhere." He wrote to specific clergy who cautioned him to go easy in the struggle for the civil rights of African Americans, but he also addressed the larger community who watched and waited. The community knew from his response that the larger struggle for justice would not end. While King's imprisonment was a momentary setback, his response to that imprisonment testifies to the vision of God's justice.

Go to Dark Gethesmane

The hymn "Go to Dark Gethsemane" speaks of Jesus' agonizing prayer in the garden. It tells of Jesus' impending crucifixion and invites us to journey to the cross with him as far as we possibly can. A great injustice takes place in the arrest, trial, and torture of Jesus. The Crucifixion becomes resurrection as God turns the wisdom of the world upside down, but we cannot skip over the injustice Jesus suffers in the meantime. If God did not believe the world worth redeeming, the story would have ended much differently. Jesus would have died between two thieves and we would no more know his name today than the names of those two thieves. Despite the world's injustice, God loves the world to the point of redeeming and transforming it. Whatever else we believe and do as Christians, the redemptive love of God in Christ remains a basic theological conviction as we go forth in our mission.

Unlike "Love Divine, All Loves Excelling," the hymn "Go to Dark Gethsemane" is not on any top-ten list of frequently requested songs. James Montgomery's words are solemn and sober. The hymn demands a slow tempo so that the words can be digested. The tune, written in a minor key by Richard Redhead, makes the words more poignant and powerful. In the hymn, we journey with Jesus from the garden of Gethsemane to the empty tomb.

James Montgomery was the son of a Moravian minister who died doing mission work in the West Indies. He was born in 1771 in Scotland. His family hoped that he would become a Moravian minister; instead, he became a poet, writer, and newspaper editor. He spent time in jail for expressing opinions that dissented from the official views of the British royalty. One of those jail terms occurred because he had criticized some judges who had banned a protest. Montgomery did not limit his activities to the newspaper. He traveled widely to speak and gain support for missionary work. He campaigned for the abolition of slavery and sought safer working conditions and equipment for chimney sweeps, a dangerous occupation at the time.

An Interruption

Dick Van Dyke and the merry band of chimney sweeps in the movie *Mary Poppins* notwithstanding, the work of chimney sweeps was not easy. Chimneys appeared in England around 1200 but were not common in houses until the sixteenth and seventeenth centuries. Before that, open fires simply burned on the floors of houses. Coal eventually replaced wood as a fuel, which caked chimneys with soot and deposited a flammable substance called creosote inside them. After the Great Fire of London in 1666, new laws required safer chimney design and cleaning. Master chimney sweeps bought young boys from their parents and from orphanages to train them to become sweeps. While adult master sweeps cleaned the chimneys before 1666, chimney designs after 1666 were smaller than earlier and older chimneys. Instead of the master sweep cleaning the chimney, boys climbed inside them to dislodge the soot. These boys usually began work at the age of six or seven. The dangerous work included the possibility of fire or getting stuck in the chimney flue and suffocating. Another working hazard was known as chimney sweep cancer. In 1775, people became aware of the problems faced by chimney sweeps and began to work for change. Organized campaigns to reform the laws were undertaken over the next twenty years. In 1875, a hundred years after reform began and a mechanical means of cleaning chimneys was developed, an Act of Parliament ended the work of chimney sweeps.

James Montgomery worked on behalf of the children who were either apprenticed or sold to chimney sweeps. Through his newspaper editorials and speeches, Montgomery became a voice for the voiceless. Underlying his activism was his Christian belief in God's grace and love. Montgomery and the Moravians traced their roots to Jan Hus, who was deemed a heretic and burned at the stake in 1415. Hus is sometimes called the *original* Protestant because he challenged the church with his belief that the Bible and the liturgy should exist in the language of the people and that the church needed other reforms. Count Nikolaus von Zinzendorf, another influential Moravian, made a lasting impact on John Wesley. Moravian Christians ordered their lives on the principle that their first loyalty was to God; all else was secondary. As a result of such beliefs, Moravians experienced persecution from governments who did not like the Moravian protests about governmental injustice. Throughout the Medieval period of European history, a span that began in the fifth century and ended with the fifteenth century, people believed in the divine right of kings (and the divine right of the church's kingly leadership) to govern as they chose. Moravians, and Montgomery in particular, challenged the injustices that occurred under these "divine" rulers.

Montgomery's poems and hymns address matters of injustice in subtle ways. As we read the words of "Go to Dark Gethsemane," we see sober descriptions of Holy Week's activities.

Go to dark Gethsemane, ye that feel the tempter's power;
your Redeemer's conflict see, watch with him one bitter hour.
Turn not from his griefs away; learn of Jesus Christ to pray.

Montgomery hides a question in this stanza: What causes Jesus grief? How would you answer that question? Montgomery's life directs us to the answer. The injustice of the world causes Jesus to weep. Slavery and terrible working conditions for children cause Jesus grief.

See him at the judgment hall,
beaten, bound, reviled, arraigned;

O the wormwood and the gall!
O the pangs his soul sustained!
Shun not suffering, shame, or loss;
learn of Christ to bear the cross.

In your mind's eye see Jesus' arrest and the ways his captors mock him. Imagine the humiliation of having clothing ripped off and being beaten prior to an appearance before Pontius Pilate—and then the Roman flogging, the crown of thorns, and other punishment. Montgomery's description of Jesus "beaten, bound, reviled, arraigned" and "the pangs his soul sustained" show us reality, but again a question hides in this stanza: Why? Why treat the Son of God with such injustice? He is, after all, the King of kings with divine rights far greater than those rulers who punish and come after him. Justice is absent, and Montgomery's plaintive words make this clear.

The fourth stanza of the hymn points us to action:

Early hasten to the tomb
where they laid his breathless clay;
all is solitude and gloom.
Who has taken him away?
Christ is risen! He meets our eyes;
Savior, teach us so to rise.

Christ rises from the injustice and hatred that led to crucifixion to the fullness of justice and love that we meet in the Resurrection. He rises from the efforts of those who love their own power and seek to gain more. How else do we explain the behavior of the chief priests who wish to rid their world of someone who challenges their authority in the Temple? How else do we understand the behavior of Pontius

Pilate to satisfy the crowd's desire for blood and thus avoid yet another bad report to his military superiors? Herod is another character who wants to solidify his power and avoid losing his position.

These major figures in the story play the power game and believe in a Golden Rule—"The one who has the most gold rules"—that differs from the one espoused by Jesus. Montgomery then adds the final phrase, "Savior, teach us so to rise." If our lives reflect Christ and if we die and rise with Christ as our baptismal vows and scripture say, then we also rise from the injustice of the world to a deeper sense of God's justice for creation. Christ calls us to rise so that God's justice may be realized through acts of love, mercy, and compassion.

Envisioning Justice

The questions at the end of earlier weeks are intended to help us see injustice more clearly in the world. We recognize injustice when we respond to a matter by saying, "That isn't right" or "That is not fair." The cry of injustice begins in our preschool years when we are not treated the way we want to be treated. In elementary school we learn that our actions have consequences, sometimes widespread. Perhaps our sharpest cries of injustice call out during our adolescent years when our vision is sharp and perception cuts through the polite veneers of society. Adolescence and young adulthood focus our vision further allowing us to comprehend social issues at basic levels of right and wrong.

But then a time comes when our hearts no longer see and our spirits no longer perceive injustice. The responsibilities of work and family temper our vision. We shrug and say, "It is what it is." We decline offers to act on behalf of causes that once engaged and excited us. We feel the constraints of time. We tire of the fight. Our sense of right and wrong becomes calcified in a way similar to the hardening of our arterial walls during middle age. Many of us face that reality.

How do we deal with our sense of feeling overwhelmed by the need but uninterested or unenergized in working for change? How do we begin to see with deeper eyes the injustice of the world and to act in ways that will change it?

Begin with prayer to discover justice through reading scripture. In the sixteenth century a soldier named Ignatius, son of the Basque nobleman Don Beltrán Yañez de Oñez y Loyola, was wounded in the Battle of Pampeluna in 1521. While recovering, Ignatius read a devotional life of Christ and experienced a transformation. Ignatius began praying for seven hours a day, usually in a cave. While praying, he began making notes and started to create a series of spiritual exercises or meditative prayers organized into four weeks. He devoted himself to God's work. Eventually Ignatius formed the Society of Jesus (Jesuits), and the pope approved this monastic order in 1540.

As scripture shaped the life of Ignatius of Loyola, so I invite you to let the Bible inform your understanding of justice. Begin by reading Amos 5:24 slowly. Read the verse again, letting it become your prayer. Let a sense of justice flow within you. Draw a picture of this flow of justice. What does this mean for the world?

Now read Micah 6:8 slowly. What do you sense in the words "to do justice, and to love kindness, and to walk humbly with your God"? What words would you use to describe your response to this verse? How would you describe justice to other people? How would you begin to describe justice for the world? Read Isaiah 1:17 slowly and prayerfully. What do these words inspire in you?

Life today is far from God's dream for the world. We know that much in the world is not just or righteous or morally good. Systems of oppression weigh heavily on people, and corruption brings pain. Justice comes in seeing what is wrong in these systems and actively working to change them. Justice comes when we feed the hungry and act to change food distribution systems. Justice flows when we choose to stand with and for the voiceless and the disenfranchised. Justice demonstrates our care for God's world.

For Your Growth

Day 1. Some philosophers and theologians claim that it is easier to define injustice than it is to define justice. How would you define injustice? What images come to mind when you think about injustice?

Day 2. Read these words from "Go to Dark Gethsemane":

> Go to dark Gethsemane, ye that feel the tempter's power;
> your Redeemer's conflict see, watch with him one bitter hour.
> Turn not from his griefs away; learn of Jesus Christ to pray.

Where do you sense the most resistance or turmoil in the quest for justice among matters that are dear to you? What do you need to overcome that resistance?

Day 3. What contemporary events come to mind when you read Amos 5:24? How can your actions show others the power of justice that flows like "an everflowing stream"?

Day 4. Read Micah 6:8 slowly. Read the verse a second time. How do you sense God's call to you through this verse? Which word or brief phrase caught your attention? How do you respond to that word or phrase? How do these words from the Bible connect you to action? Repeating this exercise may confirm what you heard or thought earlier in the week—or it may point you in a new direction.

The Next Day. What injustices do you see in news reports, television stories, and newspapers? How does your congregation respond to injustice in the community? Who in your congregation shares your passion and mission for justice? What online sources help you share your understanding of God's justice with others? What social networks do you employ to make connections?

In the Days to Come. Chimney sweeps lived hard and hazardous lives; yet, many people in the seventeenth and eighteenth centuries thought that the chimney sweeps were simply part of daily life—though invisible to most. Who are the invisible people today who are taken for granted as a necessary part of daily life? How are their conditions oppressive?

Questions for Further Consideration

1. Now that you have read this week, where do you see struggles for justice in your community life? Where is injustice growing?

2. In your community what specific actions or occurrences do you recognize that cause grief to Jesus?

3. On the road to Damascus, Paul was blinded and three days later began to see a new vision of life. How is your church seeing life anew? How is justice part of the congregation's mission and vision statement?

4. How can you become more attuned to the needs of those who suffer from injustice?

For Further Involvement

The Rev. Paul Jeffrey documents poverty in the world through images and words and describes some matters of justice and our response to these issues. Consider this video from United Methodist TV.

http://www.youtube.com/watch?v=pI5MWwB7jtk

WEEK 5

Healing the World

Surely he has borne our infirmities
and carried our diseases. . . .
But he was wounded for
our transgressions. . .
And by his bruises we are healed.

—Isaiah 53:4-5

THE WORLD EXPERIENCES different forms of brokenness. As you reflect on the questions at the end of each week's readings and pursue the news-related exercises, you see brokenness in the lives of individuals, in states and nations the world over. As you journey toward Easter, you see the broken nature of humanity in the scriptures associated with the season. People come to Jesus for healing. They hear him speak about sin; he calls them to repentance. One passage, traditionally associated with Lent, recounts the death of Lazarus and the miracle in which Jesus invoked God's mercy to return Lazarus to life.

John 11 offers many rich details in the story of Lazarus, Mary, and Martha. The story is multilayered and sensory. The chapter begins with the illness of Lazarus, brother of Mary and Martha. The Gospel of John tells us that Mary "anointed the Lord with perfume and wiped his feet with her hair" (v. 2)—a side note of an event to come in the next chapter. There Mary bathes and anoints Jesus' feet with a costly perfume (John 12:1-8). If we allow our senses to respond to this scene, our eyes see Mary of Bethany washing the dusty feet of Jesus; our ears hear the conversation; our noses smell the perfume; and we feel the touch of another person. Perhaps we sense the compassion that Mary and Jesus share. The anointing of Jesus' feet is a lull in the midst of the many claims and demands that came from the crowds and followers. The relationship between Jesus and this particular family in Bethany is a devoted one, and John draws a detailed portrait of that deep connection.

After receiving the news of Lazarus's illness, Jesus delays going to Bethany. Lazarus has been dead for four days when he finally arrives. Jesus weeps at the tomb of his friend and then calls Lazarus to come out of the tomb. The Gospel says, "The dead man came out, his hands and feet bound with strips of cloth, and his face wrapped in a cloth. Jesus said to them, 'Unbind him, and let him go'" (John 11:44).

A dozen or so years ago, I entered a painful period of life—broken relationships, broken job, broken personal and professional dreams, broken spirit. During a week in which my life felt particularly shattered, I attended worship four times and heard the story of Lazarus from John 11 read aloud at each one.

I began asking the obvious questions: *What are you saying to me, God? Am I like Lazarus? I don't have any sisters. I'm far from home. Why is this passage haunting me?* For a time I felt satisfied to focus on the healing that might happen for me as it had happened for Lazarus.

In those days I worked as a book acquisitions editor, which meant that I dealt with current authors and tried to recruit new authors to write the kinds of books we wanted to publish. Flora Slosson Wuellner was one of the authors who became a gift to me in that period of life. About a month after hearing John 11 read aloud those four times, Flora and I talked about a book on healing that she was writing. I told her about hearing John 11 four times in a single week and said, "I guess God is reminding me that healing happens." "Oh, yes, you've come to a quick conclusion of truth—perhaps too quick," said Flora. "But consider another question, and don't try to answer it as quickly as you'd like: Are the binding cloths unwinding? Who is unbinding the cloths that are wrapped around you?"

Days, weeks, and months passed before I could begin to answer the question of who was unbinding the burial cloths that bound me. I went through significant introspection and conversation to discover the answers.

For ten years my work called for me to be on the road an average of one week each month. The binding cloths that Flora helped me identify were still part of my life. They did not keep me from my vocation of ministry and publishing. I met many people around the world and listened as they spoke about wounds from divorce, from childhood, from abusive relationships, and from addiction. Some received guidance for next steps. Others simply received nonjudgmental space to tell their stories, to speak about their wounds and matters that poisoned their daily lives. I prayed with a mother in Soweto, South Africa, who told me about her son who was in prison for drug possession, a conversation that connected intimately with my own family. We prayed for each other and for those we knew and loved in prison. I listened to and prayed with an evangelical publisher whose daughter was leaving an abusive marriage.

At a Christian book event, I met Naomi Levy, a conservative rabbi. As we talked, she told me about the murder of her father and her faith journey as she struggled to deal with it. We shared other stories of faith in the midst of crises. Rabbi Levy tells a part of her story in *To Begin Again: The Journey toward Comfort, Strength, and Faith in Difficult Times*. Though I was not looking for anything beyond a successful book promotional event, I received grace in that conversation.

Healing happens, but healing does not happen on our terms or on our schedule. Our prayer for healing of a physical disease may be answered as healing of an emotional wound. Our prayer for physical healing may result in healing of a broken relationship. We do not manipulate God. So we pray for healing, and we wait. What do we do while we wait? Sitting passively is not a wise choice; life moves quickly. Sitting passively also does disservice to our understanding of God's redeeming love for the world. Even when wounded and needy, we can speak of God's love and grace and act with compassion, becoming conduits of God's healing love. No matter our condition, we live and act in faith and in hope, maintaining the long perspective of God's grace.

An Interruption

Before we consider our role in offering healing to others, I invite you to think about the meaning of health and healing. I am indebted to Howard Clinebell, one of the eminent teachers and authors of pastoral care resources, for ways to think about healing. Clinebell offers this definition:

> *Well being, wholeness,* and *wellness* . . . all mean whole-person health. This involves balanced, mutually enhancing interplay among your mind, body, and spirit; between your work and play; and in your key relationships with other people and your community; with plants and animals in the natural world; and, most important of all, with God.[6]

Clinebell identifies facets of wholeness and health: spirit, body, mind, work, play, intimate relationships, community relationships, and the environment.

Howard Clinebell's understanding of well-being began with his interpretation of Jesus' words in John 10:10: "I came that they may have life, and have it abundantly." Clinebell translated those last words as "life in all its fullness." He believed that salvation embraced the whole person and that, among other aspects of his ministry, Jesus wanted people to live spiritually empowered and holistic lives. Clinebell attempted to say with a pastoral care voice what John Wesley said in a preacher's voice: We are going on toward perfection, toward a wholeness of life that we find only in God.

If we are going *toward* wholeness and perfection, we also know that we are not there yet. No one lives the perfect life. News reports show us the imperfections of our leaders and celebrities, and we know our own limitations. No matter our wounds, Jesus invites us to extend his healing to others.

Wounds and Scars

In the tenth century, an Armenian monk known as Gregory of Narek (born Krikor Narekatsi) wrote a collection of prayers known as the *Book of Lamentations*. This title comes not because of the prayers' sadness but because they cry out from Gregory's soul. He came from a Christian household, the son of a bishop. Gregory experienced abundance for much of his life. He wrote the *Book of Lamentations* from a sense of loss concerning his health and, yet, his prayers demonstrate faith in God's ultimate victory. His writings in the years before his death are comparable to *The City of God* by Saint Augustine of Hippo. Both theologians are writing at a time when their cultures are shattered. Gregory laments his own unworthiness and ingratitude before God's grace and goodness. The ninety-five prayers in the collection have been copied, published, and distributed continuously since the year 1001. The earliest known manuscript of the collection is dated 1173 and is in the Matenadaran collection at the Armenian Church Center in Etchmiadzin, Armenia.

Gregory's physical and spiritual condition comes to the forefront throughout the prayers. We may imagine his emotional disease in seeing his culture crumble. We do not know the specific ailments or diseases that caused him pain. The prayers plead for healing, and he begs God to be a healer rather than a judge. Despite his ill health, he lives in an assurance of grace:

> Every part of my body from head to toe is unhealthy
> and beyond the help of physicians.
> But you, merciful, beneficent, blessed
> long-suffering, immortal king,
> hear the prayers of my embattled heart for mercy
> When I cry to you, "Lord,"
> in my time of need.
> (Prayer 18, Section K)

Gregory's physical condition, though a prominent part of the prayers, did not stop him from praying or teaching seminarians at the monastery in Narek. Indeed, his collection of prayers became a course in prayer and meditation. His prayers weave basic concerns with biblical wisdom and refer to many Bible passages. Gregory prayed that, despite his illness, his words would teach many people:

> Here is my profession of faith....
> What I have discoursed upon before,
>   I set forth again,
> these written instructions and interpretations
> for the masses of different nations.
> I offer these prayers of intercession.
> (Prayer 34, Section A)

Reading the prayers of Gregory of Narek brings us in contact with the spiritual concerns of a Christian brother from another century, and we discover and connect with our own wounds and concerns. (I read and pray one section each day as part of my daily devotional practice.) Gregory's illness did not keep him from expressing spiritual depth, anguish, and assurance. Though the heart and the soul of Gregory were wounded, his wounds did not distract the saint from showing forgiveness, healing, mercy, love, and grace.

About ten centuries after Gregory, Henri J. M. Nouwen wrote *The Wounded Healer*, in which he voices the concerns of many people who feel called to ministry but not to the traditional role of professional minister. Nouwen helped many people recognize their woundedness, which allows them to care for others who are wounded. Nouwen did not allow his wounds to keep him from offering healing wisdom to others. Nouwen's basic premise: A person who is not wounded in some way will have no depth of regard for the wounds of others. Nouwen used spiritual and psychological insight to reveal the wounded nature of the world and to show that we follow in the path of the wounded Christ who offers healing to all. *The Wounded Healer* has helped many people clarify their calling to ministry.

In words from the book of James: "If a brother or sister is naked and lacks daily food, and one of you says to them, 'Go in peace; keep warm and eat your fill,' and yet you do not supply their bodily needs, what is the good of that?" (2:15-16). I imagine that James addresses someone who has not experienced nakedness or hunger or other forms of physical poverty, but who lives in a state of spiritual poverty.

Christian disciples live with the example of the wounded healer. Isaiah 53 describes the Suffering Servant in this way:

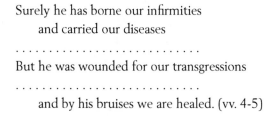

> Surely he has borne our infirmities
>   and carried our diseases
>
> . . . .
>
> But he was wounded for our transgressions
>
> . . . .
>
>   and by his bruises we are healed. (vv. 4-5)

Echoing the theme in Isaiah, the author of First Peter writes, "'He himself bore our sins' in his body on the cross, so that we might die to sins and live for righteousness; 'by his wounds you have been healed'" (2:24, NIV).

For two years I walked two miles each way to work every day. I lived in the urban core of the city, and on those walks I met men and women who were homeless. Some of the regulars on my route began to recognize me as I walked by. I learned some of their names, personalities, and personal histories. One day while I was on a run, a man stopped me and asked for food. I told him that I didn't have any food with me but that we were three blocks from my church where food was available. We talked more, and I invited him to come to the church. "No, you have blessed me by taking the time to look me in the face and talk directly to me. Most people don't do that. Thank you." He went away. I wondered if I had met an angel. The author of Hebrews says, "Do not forget to show hospitality to strangers, for by so doing some people have shown hospitality to angels without knowing it" (13:2, NIV).

I do not intend to romanticize urban life. One morning, I was attacked by four adolescents. While I was on the ground being kicked, someone yelled at the attackers and called the police. The stranger returned and sat with me until the police arrived, and I was taken away in an ambulance. Later, I stopped at each house on the block, but I could find no one who admitted to being the anonymous person. I remain grateful to this stranger. After the assault I did not turn away from life in the urban core of the city, and I continue to pray for those four unknown assailants.

Who are the wounded around you? How do you recognize them? Are they world-weary or worn down by the weight of too many changes in life, such as economic disruption, illness, or deep-seated conflict? Are they weighed down by conditions that they did not choose or create? Have their spiritual or emotional wounds led to other hurts? What are their needs? To identify the wounded in the world, begin to listen to the stories of others. Notice both what they do and do not talk about.

There Is a Balm in Gilead

I bought a recording of the baritone Paul Robeson shortly after his death. My musical preferences at the time were small jazz groups, select rock groups, and some opera. I had not heard Robeson prior to that recording but was intrigued by his obituary—African American, scholar, athlete, lawyer, actor, activist. The recording included "There Is a Balm in Gilead," and I was astonished by the depth and richness of Robeson's baritone. After the third or fourth time I listened to the recording, I began to pay attention to the words of the spiritual. They respond to a question from the book of Jeremiah:

Is there no balm in Gilead?
  Is there no physician there?
Why then has the health of my poor people
  not been restored? (8:22).

In case you do not have a recording of Paul Robeson singing this song, here are the words:

Chorus
There is a balm in Gilead
to make the wounded whole;
there is a balm in Gilead
to heal the sin-sick soul.

Verse
Sometimes I feel discouraged,
and think my work's in vain.
But then the Holy Spirit
revives my soul again.

Repeat Chorus
If you can't preach like Peter,
if you can't pray like Paul,
just tell the love of Jesus,
and say he died for all.

Whenever we sing this hymn, we may identify some sort of healing balm that came from Gilead, and we also connect this balm with the healing and redeeming love of Jesus Christ. Come with me a little deeper into the history and meaning of the text.

We first encounter Gilead in Genesis 31:21. It is located east of the Jordan River in the mountainous region of the Hashemite Kingdom of Jordan. Gilead's neighbors included Bashan, Moab, and Ammon.

Jacob deceives his father-in-law, true to his nature as a trickster. Jacob, his wives, and family flee his father-in-law, Laban, and journey toward the hill country of Gilead. Rachel, Laban's daughter, deceives both her father and her husband after stealing her father's sacred vessels (called "the household gods" in Genesis). When Laban realizes that Jacob has deceived him, Laban goes after him. The men meet again in the hill country of Gilead. At Gilead, Laban and Jacob speak truth to each other and reconcile. They make a covenant and erect a stone marker as evidence of that covenant. The word *Gilead* itself testifies to this covenant. In Hebrew the word *Gil* means "joy." The word *ad* means "eternal," "forever," or "eternity." Putting together the words *Gil* and *ad* (or "joy" and "eternal") lead to the compound *Gilead*, which can mean a memorial marker for eternity.

Remember that God believes the world is worth saving. The primary image we have to remind us of salvation is the cross. Think of the cross as a Gilead. The cross becomes a marker that reminds us of the covenant made between God and humanity. As the cross is elevated or emphasized in our understanding of God's love, we know that our wounds are healed by Christ. We affirm the redemptive love represented in the cross, and we invite others to see the cross in this new light.

The words of "There Is a Balm in Gilead" encourage me for the long-haul journey of faith. The anonymous hymn writer inspires us to use our gifts—no matter our age or condition or state of faith: "Just tell the love of Jesus, and say he died for all." In fasting from apathy, we also fast from those inner voices that tell us we cannot offer healing to others. We *can* offer healing and, despite our own wounds, we must.

Ways to Offer Healing

How do we offer healing from our own wounded experience? Who needs healing, and where do we begin?

I invite you to consider James 1:27 as a way to think about offering healing to a wounded world: "Religion that God our Father accepts as pure and faultless is this: to look after orphans and widows in their distress and to keep oneself from being polluted by the world" (NIV).

In ancient Israel, when a woman became a widow she would either move in with other family members or become an outcast. Israel's patriarchal society meant that the death of a husband became an economic and social disaster for the wife. In general, women had no legal status or the right to inherit family property except in special cases. When we read about widows in the Bible, many of the references speak in terms of the justice or injustice of their condition. The Torah offers guidance and legal protection for widows. The prophets decry the exploitation of widows. (See Isa. 1:17; Jer. 7:5-7; Ezek. 22:6-7; Zech. 7:8-14; Mal. 3:5.) Psalm 72 speaks of the king's deliverance of the needy "and those who have no helper" (vv. 12-14). In the Gospel of Matthew, Jesus says, ""Do not think that I have come to abolish the law or the prophets; I have come not to abolish but to fulfill" (5:17).

When offering healing to others, begin with widows and orphans. While our culture is not so patriarchal that women cannot inherit property, widows and orphans continue to face unique obstacles. We first need to recognize the basis for widowhood and the orphan state—death.

Death is the wound that everyone fears. Our human imaginations—whether formed by faith or the lack of it—cannot fathom existence beyond the present one. Because we cannot penetrate the mystery of death, we shy away from it. We avoid talking about death, and we frequently avoid those whose loved ones have died. Often we do not know what to say to those who grieve and mourn. We simply feel uncomfortable around death.

Widows and orphans feel the sting keenly. They face daily reminders of a loved one who has died. Death disrupts the lives of surviving family members. They face emotional wounds and significant changes in life. Their material lives may also change as a result of loss of income or economic upheaval. When we avoid or turn away from widows and orphans, we fail them and we fail Christ.

Look around. There are widows and orphans nearby. Listen to them. Listen deeply. What messages come from their hearts? How can you help them so that they will not be exploited in some way or another? Remember that exploitation today may come in various forms. One means of exploitation the prophets decried was usury, which we see today in the form of unsecured loans available through a television or web ad or at the "payday" lending center on the corner. That widow you know may need $200 to pay utility bills, and because she borrowed from one of these sources she now pays $200 plus an exorbitant rate of interest that is far above the interest rates of credit cards and other loans. Could you and your church establish a form of credit union that could make emergency funds available within the community? Could you begin a prayer ministry? What action might you take to stand with those who are being exploited or taken advantage of?

In Southern Africa children are left orphans because of the AIDS epidemic. Many underfunded mission organizations work to make a difference in the lives of these children. How might you begin to care for these orphans?

Widows and orphans need healing. The inhabitants of our world need healing of body, mind, and spirit. Our world needs healing of relationships between individuals and nations. We meet wounded people every day; all need to receive the gifts of healing. Our journey through Lent connects us more intimately with this need and with Jesus Christ.

Jesus began his public ministry, according to the Gospel of Mark, with deeds of healing. In the synagogue on a sabbath, he heals a man with an unclean spirit. (See Mark 1:21-28.) He then leaves the synagogue and visits the home of Simon and Andrew to heal Simon's mother-in-law. Then Jesus continues to offer healing to the crowd of people who gather around the house (Mark 1:29-34). The broken nature of the world continues to our time, and we follow the example of Jesus by offering healing to those we meet.

For Your Growth

Day 1. Who came to mind as you read about healing this week? Did you pray for healing of that situation?

Day 2. Saint Benedict wrote his Rule in the sixth century as a way to help Christian disciples center their lives in Christ.

Benedict proposed that the Rule become a "school for the Lord's service," and countless Christian disciples have grown in faith by heeding Benedict's instruction. In the prologue Benedict writes the following: "Listen carefully, my child, to your master's precepts, and incline the ear of your heart (Prov. 4:20)." What does the phrase, "the ear of your heart," represent for you?

Draw a picture of the ear of your heart. How would you explain the art or the phrase to your church? Listen now with the ear of your heart to the cries of those who are wounded. What do you hear? Whose wound calls for your attention? Whose suffering invites your gifts of healing?

Day 3. Both Gregory of Narek and Henri Nouwen wrote about their wounds in ways that helped others receive healing. Many years ago one of my friends was raped. In the years since that horrible experience, she has helped other women deal with the effects of rape. It is her way to offer space in which healing may happen. I know also that sometimes people do not speak of their wounds because of safety concerns. In the privacy and safety of your study or reading area, identify your wounds. How do they inform the way you perceive and reach out to others? When you see people with wounds like yours, do you respond with compassion and mercy?

Day 4. Return to your list of news stories or look at today's news reports. Where do you sense a need for healing? What healing might you offer?

The Next Day. Take time to reflect on the words of "There Is a Balm in Gilead." What monument to eternal joy are you erecting by offering healing to others?

In the Days to Come. Pray the words of "What Wondrous Love Is This"; praise God for believing in the world, loving it, and offering salvation through the wounded and healing Christ. After your prayer time, consider other needs that you have identified throughout the reading of this book. What issues or problems seem to demand your energy? Which issues or problems seem to have suggested steps toward solution of the matter? Take the first steps to move your solution toward reality. Go on that visit. Make that telephone call. Send that e-mail. Write that letter. Talk to others at your church who may share a similar concern. Start the healing service or the weekend backpacks for hungry children project or begin to speak prophetically about injustice in your community. Taking action is more satisfying than living with the inertia or paralysis of analysis.

Questions for Further Consideration

1. What have you learned about healing from your reading this week?

2. How do you respond to Howard Clinebell's understanding of well-being and wholeness? Why would Clinebell include the environment or the earth in his understanding of wholeness and well-being?

3. How do you recognize your own wounds? How can your wounds offer healing to others?

4. Who are the wounded in your community? What are their needs?

For Further Involvement

Consider what this United Methodist TV video about a drive-through prayer ministry teaches about healing.

http://www.youtube.com/watch?v=ndReA6liqsU

WEEK 6

Refining Friendship

*Love your enemies and pray for those who
persecute you.*

—MATTHEW 5:44

MY FATHER OPERATED a small corner grocery store in the
industrial town of Hopewell, Virginia. The intersection of Fifteenth and Atlantic in Hopewell revealed the aspirations of
immigrants from the time when the town grew from a village
on the James and Appomattox Rivers with roots that reached
back to 1613 to become a small manufacturing center with
access to a deep port and the Atlantic Ocean. Diagonally
across the street from our store was an Armenian-owned confectionary. Opposite the confectionary was an Italian-owned
tavern. Next door to the tavern was a Greek barbershop. On
the fourth corner a Turkish man operated a grocery store.
Down the street a Syrian family ran a neighborhood grocery store. That was years ago and the old neighborhood has

undergone many changes. Today a Korean family operates our old Armenian grocery and other immigrants have arrived in the town.

The world felt different then. The United States and the Soviet Union were in a continual geopolitical conflict called the Cold War that lasted for more than forty years. This war of political ideologies involved competing understandings of nation and government. The rhetoric of the era divided everything into the categories of "us" and "them." But life can never be so clearly defined by categories like these.

One Sunday my father spoke quietly about something that happened during the week at the store. An Armenian sailor, a citizen of the Soviet Union who worked on a Greek freighter, jumped ship in Hopewell. He knew enough English to search for an Armenian name in the telephone directory. He found our family grocery, came to the store, and asked my father to help him settle in the United States. Hagop, which was not his real name, simply wanted the freedom and opportunities extended by the United States. My father said, "I did what any son of an immigrant would do. I helped him. It's what we do as Americans and as Christians." He talked about sharing wealth and resources with those in need, helping people, and finding ways to connect with those who had less than we had. "You boys go to church," my father said. Because my father and I were both named George, he addressed me in his usual way, "Big Boy, isn't that what the Bible says to do?" One of the rental houses my father owned was vacant, so Hagop stayed in that rental house for a month while he looked for work. Our family fed him and helped him begin a new and productive life. Hagop moved to Richmond, Virginia, married, and had a family. He worked in a pharmaceutical firm in Richmond and died an American citizen. Hagop and my parents were friends until my parents' deaths, and Hagop and I remained in touch until his death. I knew of other Armenians who became United States citizens because my father did not turn them away when they jumped ship. He also helped economic immigrants from states along the East Coast who came to Hopewell in search of work. What made the story about Hagop so memorable for me was that this was one of the few times I heard my father speak directly about Christianity. My father went to Armenian church services once every three months or so and did not seem to care much for the message. Even so, he had a sense of Christian behavior and expectation, especially generosity toward strangers.

An Interruption

Today my father would be subject to arrest for his actions. He acted from a sense of compassion and understanding. My parents were first-generation Armenians in this country. Their families settled wherever they could. They worked hard and found ways to survive economically and culturally. None of my grandparents spoke English well; however, they insisted that their children complete high school and go to college and that their grandchildren enter the professions of medicine or law (or become Armenian priests).

The culture of the United States in my father's lifetime differed from the culture today. My father lived with the pervasive fear of the possibility of a nuclear attack and retaliatory nuclear response. Given that possibility, fear was an underlying part of life. The actions of the United States and the Soviet Union during the Soviet missile installation in Cuba fertilized that Cold War fear. Fear has grown exponentially since those days, especially after the attacks of September 11, 2001.

During the last twenty years, I have befriended Armenians who escaped genocide in Azerbaijan during the 1990s and found new life in the United States. The United States could use their skills as engineers, architects, doctors, dentists, and chemists. The September 11 attacks destroyed the sense of refuge these Armenian immigrants had in the United States. Fear caused people to identify these newcomers as terrorists. Imagine escaping religious persecution in one land to experience personal attacks in another land because of physical appearance. Fear has terrible effects on people, and it is little wonder the Bible refers so often to casting out fear.

The Meaning of Friendship

What does friendship mean to you? Many preschool children make friends quickly and come home from day care or the playground and tell their parents about their new best friends. In adolescence, making friends is a serious matter. Adolescents hope to choose the right people, the right group, or even the right mix of friends. Follow the arc of friendship from adolescence to midlife. In young adulthood and on toward midlife, our groups of acquaintances expand as we connect with neighbors, coworkers, and persons with similar vocations. The number of our acquaintances grows through participation in church life, Sunday school classes, and small-group studies. We may enlarge our circle of friends by participating in softball or bowling leagues, running groups or garden cooperatives, stamp-collecting groups, book clubs, or fantasy football leagues. Our list of acquaintances grows even larger when we join social media groups like Facebook and Twitter, reconnecting with people from previous chapters in our lives. Notice that I now use the word *acquaintance*. While we would like to consider each person we know as a friend, we do not have the same relationship with everyone we know.

As we age, friendships seem harder to make. Perhaps friendships were easier to establish in childhood and adolescence because we knew so little and our lives were open to many possibilities. With age, our opinions and convictions become firm; we may not want to deal with the many opinions among people. We also begin to see friendships end because of divorce and death.

If we were to draw circles to demonstrate our relationships with various friends, we would begin as an individual in a circle with our closest friends. These may include some family members, though not all of them. This group contains our close confidants—ones who know our dreams and hopes. They may also know a little about our history. Beyond that layer would be another circle of persons who go back to an earlier point in our lives—adolescence or childhood. Together we may remember common events but do not share confidences today. Beyond the group of old buddies is another circle of acquaintances we see in daily life. We work together. We complain about the weather or politics or the sermon. We tell one another jokes, but we don't tell this group our dreams. Our circles expand to include another group who may be the friends of coworkers and the people we know through our Sunday school class. Expanding the number of circles still more, we reach people through social media—some are friends indeed, while others we know only as digital beings.

Expanding Friendship

Making and keeping friends calls for two actions that we may not consciously recognize: (1) extending hospitality, and (2) extending support. Many books invite and urge us to become gracious, compassionate, and kind. Many authors note that the shrinking borders and boundaries around the world require better ways to offer hospitality to others. Some writers point to the traditions of hospitality in different religions. Others appeal to monastic traditions of hospitality as models for contemporary Christians.

I suggest a biblical approach to hospitality. Instead of perceiving ourselves as the ones with gifts to share, we improve hospitality when we take into account our own feelings when we receive hospitality from others. When others welcome us into their lives, we understand and accept with gratitude their hospitality. We receive from them food and drink, shelter and comfort. Hospitable people do not remind us that we eat from their plates or sit in their chairs. They make us feel comfortable, and we are grateful. Do we also feel a sense of gratitude for the opportunity to serve?

When I have traveled internationally, I have visited countries where I speak only a fraction of the language and others where I could not speak the language at all. When I did not understand the national language, someone who spoke both the national language and my own helped me. When I visited places on my own or went to restaurants, no one spoke in a louder voice if I could not understand their words. No one walked away from me and called me a derogatory name because I did not speak their language. I asked elementary questions. When I noticed cultural differences I asked about them. I was treated respectfully, though some of my questions elicited laughter.

Some of my observations mystified people. Nations develop different customs and traditions, and I find that asking questions becomes a way to learn. For example, driving through Johannesburg, South Africa, I realized that no flags flew above or in front of car dealerships like in the United States. I mentioned this to my South African companion who was surprised that a car dealer would fly a large flag in front of the business. My South African acquaintance asked if other businesses in the United States also flew flags, and my negative response puzzled him even more.

In Switzerland I met with French-speaking United Methodists from Europe and Africa. Delegates to the gathering arrived from Cameroon, Côte d'Ivoire, the Democratic Republic of the Congo, Chad, Algeria, Zimbabwe, France, the United States, and Switzerland. All the delegates stayed in a hotel that was once a convent. Our host worked hard to meet our needs and a variety of requests. During a lull in the action, I asked our Swiss host how he managed to do the work so smoothly. He smiled and said, "I am a Wesleyan. I wake up early and spend time in prayer and Bible study. Part of my prayer time includes praying for each person at this conference. I read your names from my list and ask God to direct my hands and my heart to serve each one of you as God wants."

We often identify friendship and hospitality with the actions of extroverts. Yet both friendship and hospitality begin with the inner discipline of prayer. In other words, introverts may practice friendship and hospitality as well as extroverted personalities.

The author of First John addresses a community in which traveling preachers were teaching a doctrine that contradicted the incarnation of God in Jesus Christ. The false teaching focused on the idea that Jesus was not fully human but only a spiritual projection of a human image. In the early portion of the letter, the author deals with this false teaching and then addresses what constitutes Christian community. At the end of chapter 3, John's letter tells Christians to love one another in the community of faith: "Little children, let us love, not in word or speech, but in truth and action" (3:18). These simple words call for a lifetime of understanding and action. The words connect with a passage from the letter of James: "What good is it, my brothers and sisters, if you say you have faith but do not have works?" (2:14). If we love only with our words, then our love accomplishes little. We betray the God who believes in humanity and the value of the world.

Forth in Thy Name, O Lord

Our Lenten journey brings us to the time when Jesus faces betrayal, arrest, desertion, trial, and crucifixion. Disciples and followers travel with Jesus for a period of time. They see his miracles and witness his healings. They listen as he talks about the kingdom of God, and they hear new teachings. Some of these followers he names as friends, but these friends desert Jesus when the Romans arrest him. They run and hide in fear. The disciples' actions during Holy Week do not serve as strong role models for discipleship today.

As we near the end of the journey and approach Jesus' resurrection, let us consider a hymn that does not relate directly to Lent or Easter; it is, instead, a hymn of daily life, written by Charles Wesley and published in 1749. We sing the hymn, set to the tune "Duke Street," infrequently. Some congregations reserve the singing of this hymn for Labor Day.

Forth in thy name, O Lord, I go,
my daily labor to pursue;
thee, only thee, resolved to know
in all I think or speak or do.

What is your daily labor? You and I share at least one task in common: prayer. Jesus Christ calls us to pray. Our prayers cast out fear and open us to hospitality and friendship. Our prayers give us wisdom and courage to initiate relationships, to extend grace to strangers, and to entertain angels unaware. Our daily labor in prayer encourages us to fast from apathy; to serve others, feed the hungry, challenge injustice, and be the body of Christ in the world. Every action discussed in this book begins in our prayer life. As

Christians, every action on behalf of others begins with our inner practice of prayer.

> The task thy wisdom hath assigned,
> O let me cheerfully fulfill;
> in all my works thy presence find,
> and prove thy good and perfect will.

What task has God given you? Do you sell or buy? Do you sing or act? Do you work in a factory or an office? Are you retired or just beginning to work? If Brother Lawrence could remain grounded in God while scrubbing kitchen pots and pans in a seventeenth-century monastic kitchen and Julian of Norwich could say that "all shall be well" in the midst of the bubonic plague of the fourteenth and fifteenth centuries, we also can find ways to fulfill the task at hand. Brother Lawrence and Julian (and countless Christians before and after them) found assurance, direction, and God's presence in their daily discipline of prayer.

> Thee may I set at my right hand,
> whose eyes mine inmost substance see,
> and labor on at thy command,
> and offer all my works to thee.

Can we offer all that we do to God? What would it mean if daily prayer shaped our daily work? We could then speak truth in love. We could act without fear of reprisal. As Jesus' disciples we could walk more closely with him.

> For thee delightfully employ
> whate'er thy bounteous grace hath given;
> and run my course with even joy,
> and closely walk with thee to heaven.

I invite you to use this hymn by Charles Wesley as your morning prayer. Read it slowly or sing it unaccompanied. Let the words guide your daily interaction with the world. No matter what we do, let us go forth in Jesus' name.

So What?

How do we begin to expand friendships? Where do we start in extending hospitality? The basic answer: Begin where you are. Who in your neighborhood is overlooked? Which people have difficulty communicating with you?

In some neighborhoods people's invisibility hinges on their speaking a language different from the predominant one. They may speak Spanish in a predominantly English-speaking area. Or they may speak Vietnamese in a Spanish-speaking neighborhood. They may be deaf and use American Sign Language in a neighborhood filled with talkers. They may be the last members of the World War II generation to live in an area populated by Millennials.

When my parents' generation grew up in the United States, the goal was assimilation; every immigrant child wanted to fit in and be an American. Immigrants exerted a great deal of effort to homogenize cultural differences. Many people of that generation and the next generation grieved the loss of language and cultural heritage even while they celebrated living in the United States. Today we live in a world that celebrates difference and seeks to find ways to bring diverse cultures, perspectives, and experiences to our common understanding.

As our understanding of friendship and hospitality grows, so does our awareness of those who mourn the loss of a common cultural heritage and a common experience from which to communicate. I once worked with a Chinese man who came to the United States after the Tiananmen Square protests in 1989. He told me that in one of the more effective public demonstrations, participants wore T-shirts imprinted with one number—the number in Mao Tse Tung's little red book that concerned freedom of education. Because everyone in China was required to read and study this book, everyone knew the reference number. Such a common text as the little red book makes communication easy among the more than one billion Chinese people.

The United States does not have a common reference book, which makes communication more challenging. As Christians, diversity reminds us of that significant day of Pentecost in which the gospel was communicated across cultural and language barriers. We embrace the possibility of extending hospitality and bearing witness across cultural and language barriers today.

How do you expand hospitality in your neighborhood and beyond? Maybe your church offers a safe space for children after school to study, receive tutoring, enjoy a snack, and work off their pent-up energy.

At the other end of the aging scale, what are older adults in your community experiencing? Is your congregation able to provide transportation or delivery services? Do you provide space for support groups? How can you or your congregation offer guidance for the leadership of such groups?

I have raised more questions than I have provided answers.

I do not know your community's needs. I do know that your community has needs and that you already have some of the answers. Begin to answer the questions I have asked here and trust that God is already working to help make those answers become real to people as you engage in mission and the expansion of friendship.

This week we look toward Easter. Our churches celebrate with varying services of worship that may range from revival services to a foot-washing on Holy Thursday to a Tenebrae service on Good Friday. We may not have as much time to read as we do during an ordinary week, but God continues to invite us to revise and refine our understanding of friendship to embrace the world that God believes is worth saving.

Let this be your daily prayer of blessing:

Forth in thy name, O Lord, I go,
my daily labor to pursue;
thee, only thee, resolved to know
in all I think or speak or do.

For Your Growth

Day 1. Earlier in this week's reading you were asked to consider your circles of friendships and acquaintances. Reflect now on those circles. Where do your friends fit within the different orbits? Now think about your community and the people you pass on the streets. Who in your community is missing from your circles? How would you include those who are missing? How might your church begin to include these others?

Day 2. If you participate in Holy Week services at your church, begin to notice who the visitors to your congregation are during these services. What hospitality can you extend to these visitors? How can you expand your understanding of friendship and include these visitors in the life of the community?

Day 3. In this week's reading we looked at a hymn with the words "Forth in thy name, O Lord, I go, / my daily labor to pursue." How will you extend hospitality today as part of your daily labor in the name of Jesus?

Day 4. What practices or disciplines have been most beneficial to you in your fast from apathy? What tempted you to give up? What helped you overcome that temptation? To paraphrase one of John Wesley's questions: What delivered you from an apathetic response?

The Next Day. Beyond the daily ministry of hospitality, how else do you identify your daily labor on God's behalf? How will your actions reflect your prayer and commitment to go "Forth in Thy Name, O Lord"?

In the Days to Come. How will you encourage and help others fast from their apathy? Are you currently participating in a missional interest group that is dealing with needs that you identified? If you are not, now is an excellent time to begin such a group.

Questions for Further Consideration

1. How does fear of those who differ from you affect your perception of the world?

2. How do you initiate conversations with visitors at your church?

3. When have you felt fear about someone who is different from you? How did you respond? When have you needed to be reminded that those who seem different from you in appearance are also God's children?

4. "God so loved the world that he gave his only Son, so that everyone who believes in him may not perish but may have eternal life" (John 3:16). What does this verse mean for you in terms of expanding friendship and hospitality in your congregation and neighborhood?

For Further Involvement

Hospitality supports the theme of a video created in 2012 that asks what the church will be like in eighty years. While the questions and responses come from United Methodist leaders, the video connects across the theological and church spectrum. As you watch this video, think about the ways your understanding of friendship and hospitality impacts congregational mission.

http://www.youtube.com/watch?v=9a0sSY_WYGU

The video below speaks of the gospel and the church as a movement outward for all the world, reminding us that God believes the world is indeed worth saving.

http://www.youtube.com/watch?v=Z_4u8TRorUw

Facing Resurrection

THE SEASON OF LENT is rapidly coming to an end. If you gave up meat for Lent, you may celebrate the Resurrection by eating lamb or ham. If you gave up chocolate for Lent, you may eat a chocolate bunny rabbit for breakfast after an Easter sunrise service. But I hope the first moments of Easter mean more than that to you.

In this book I have invited you into a nontraditional kind of fast—the invitation to give up apathy. I have encouraged you to replace your apathy with an attitude of compassion as you continue to seek ways to connect your inner spiritual practices with the actions of faith and discipleship. If you began your fast from apathy because you know that God believes that the world is worth saving, then please do not end your fast on Easter.

The resurrected Christ frees us from our apathy so we can serve others. Our service can take many forms: feeding the hungry, clothing the naked, visiting those in prison, tending the sick, challenging injustice, and living as the body of Christ in the world. Teresa of Ávila, a sixteenth-century mystic, wrote a poem of devotion that begins in this way:

Christ has no body but yours,
No hands, no feet on earth but yours.

How you and I become the hands and feet of Christ—the body of Christ on earth—helps determine the world's response to the redeeming love and grace of God. We have nothing to offer the world unless we offer Christ through our actions.

Return with me to the words of Pope Leo the Great, which I quoted in the preface:

> Let us adorn our fasting with works of mercy. Spend in good deeds what you withdraw from superfluity. Our fast must be turned into a banquet for the poor. Let us devote time and effort to the underprivileged, the widow and the orphan; let us show sympathy to the afflicted and reconcile the estranged; provide lodging for the wanderer and relieve the oppressed; give clothing to the naked and cherish the sick.

Let's turn our fast from apathy into a feast of care and compassion for the widows and orphans, the hungry and needy, those in need of healing and hope. We do this for one simple reason:

God believes that the world is worth saving.
Amen, amen, and amen.

A Postscript about Spirituality Types

Many books focus on different methods and types of prayer. By reading those books we learn that some prayers are read or spoken aloud. Some prayers are memorized. Others are spontaneous. Some authors separate prayer types into voiced or vocal prayer, meditation, and contemplation; but we need not stop the list here. As Brother Lawrence reminds us, we pray through painting or music or making bread. We pray through our deeds of mercy to people who are homeless. We pray through our deeds of justice as we encourage others to hear the cries of the needy.

Some people appreciate the designations of *introvert* and *extrovert* spirituality and note that introverts pray in one way and extroverts prefer another. Those descriptive terms come from the Myers-Briggs test. However, that test was never intended as a tool to define or assess spirituality. At best, the insights gained from the Myers-Briggs Type Indicator help some people speak in shorthand about personality traits and the connection between personality traits and spirituality.

Our spirituality, however, is not so easily understood that we can describe it simply as introvert and extrovert and then move on to another subject. In her book titled *Discover Your Spiritual Type*, Corinne Ware connects personality traits with spirituality. She builds upon the foundational work of Urban T. Holmes III to develop a structure to support our exploration of spirituality. Dr. Ware uses a circle with multiple points that she refers to as the Spirituality Wheel to show the complexity of spirituality types. Imagine a compass. At the North Pole is head or intellectual spirituality. At the South Pole is heart or affective spirituality. Head spirituality emphasizes knowing God through logic and rationality, whereas heart spirituality emphasizes knowing God through feeling and intuition.

In addition to the North-South Poles, every compass has an East-West axis, and here that axis helps us think more deeply about spirituality. To the East is kataphatic spirituality, which we may best summarize as an affirmative or positive way to think about God. If you envision the face of Jesus when you pray, then you are demonstrating kataphatic spirituality. On the West Pole of our compass is apophatic spirituality. Apophatic spirituality thinks about God by emptying the mind of all images and focusing on the holy mystery of God. *The Cloud of Unknowing*, a spiritual classic written by an English monk in the fourteenth century, offers one example of this kind of spirituality. Dr. Ware helps us consider prayer and spirituality by illustrating these four poles. She helps us note the different points that compose our spiritual lives.

If you would like to know more about prayer and personality types, read Corinne Ware's book and take the self-test, which is easily taken and scored.

The book contains options for use. Individuals may take the self-test and score it and grow in awareness as a result of the test. Ware also offers a section for congregational use. She makes it possible to test the entire congregation or to use the test with a small group. Gaining insight into the spirituality of a congregation may enable the church to grow in mission and ministry, to look at new possibilities for witness and service, and to let go of those programs that no longer fit the congregation.

Discover Your Spiritual Type: A Guide to Individual and Congregational Growth, by Corinne Ware, is published by The Alban Institute and available from the usual booksellers or from the publisher (www.alban.org).

Notes

1. Pius Parsch, *The Church's Year of Grace*, trans. William G. Heidt (Collegeville, MN: Liturgical Press, 1959), 1:103–104.

2. Brother Lawrence, *The Practice of the Presence of God and the Spiritual Maxims* (Mineola, NY: Dover Publications, Inc., 2005), 61–62.

3. Ibid, 61.

4. Ibid, 16.

5. Howard Clinebell, *Anchoring Your Well Being: Christian Wholeness in a Fractured World* (Nashville, TN: Upper Room Books, 1997), 18.

For Leaders of Small Groups

BECAUSE THE TOPICS covered in *A World Worth Saving* connect with the season of Lent and suggest either a small-group or whole-congregation study, you may be leading such a small group. Studying a book with others often gives corporate insights that may be less evident with a solo reading. Think of this time together as a gift from God.

I offer three general comments:

1. Read the book and familiarize yourself with the content. Get a sense of the content and the approach.

2. Consider the purpose of the study. Why are you studying this book in a small-group setting? What do you hope others will gain from the time together? Are you engaged in the study because it seemed like something good to do during Lent or because the congregation always selects a book for the season? Are you engaged in the study to move toward new action in ministry and mission? Are you engaged in the study to help Christian disciples work together to grow more deeply in their witness to the world? Take time to clarify your purpose in leading a

121

group and your expectations for the group. If you wish, you may list the expectations and hopes and present them to the group.

3.   Think about the group participants. What do you know about their Christian experience? What do you know about their life away from church? Use what you know about the participants to prepare for each session. You may discover, for example, that your leadership style of group conversation does not fit the group's expectation of classroom lecture. You may need to mix lecture and group conversation or invite a large group to form as pairs or triads for conversation after a lecture portion.

Here is a simple pattern for meeting as a group.

Gather

People will talk as they enter the room. They will also begin to shift their focus to the purpose of gathering. They may begin to talk about personal concerns or concerns for the congregation. Listen to their concerns.

Open with Prayer

Pray aloud or ask someone in the group to pray aloud. Thank God for bringing together the group from many different places in life. Ask God's Spirit to guide your teaching and learning together. You may light a candle before the prayer, telling the group that the candle symbolizes the Holy Spirit's presence. Leave the candle lit throughout the session.

Discuss the Week's Reading

Ask the participants if any words or ideas seemed strange or needed clarification. Give a brief overview of the content and then discuss together the questions at the end of the week's reading. Other questions you may wish to ask:

- What new insight did you gain about _____ (apathy, hunger, serving, healing, justice, friendship)?

- How does this week's conversation help you think differently about the hymn _____ discussed in the reading?

- As you follow the news, how do you hear God guiding you in ministry? What nudges indicate God's calling you to act in a new way or to respond to an injustice?

- After reading this week's content, what change do you seek in your life or in the life of this community?

- How is your relationship with God changing as a result of reading this week's material (or this book)?

Share Prayer Concerns

Ask participants to offer their concerns aloud so the entire group can continue in prayer for these concerns in the days to come after the group session.

Close with Prayer

Pray together, naming the group concerns. Give thanks to God for gathering the group together and for guiding the conversation.

Scatter

Thank the participants for coming to the session. As individuals came from many different places in life to become a group, so participants return to their separate paths and spaces. Extinguish the candle and go in peace.

About the Author

GEORGE DONIGIAN is the pastor of Monaghan United Methodist Church in Greenville, South Carolina. He is an ordained elder and member of the Virginia Conference of The United Methodist Church. He also works as an editorial consultant.

Donigian grew up in a corner grocery store, worked on a garbage truck in college, in a sandpaper factory before seminary, and served as pastor of a number of United Methodist churches (including a four-point circuit) in Virginia prior to moving into the publishing world.

Donigian's foray into publishing included the following pursuits: acquisition editor for leadership, small-group, and program resources, Upper Room Books; director of trade marketing, Upper Room Books; and team leader-editor-publisher-creative director, Discipleship Resources.

CPSIA information can be obtained at www.ICGtesting.com
Printed in the USA
LVOW11s0608290115

424760LV00002B/2/P

9 780835 812115